CHILDREN OF POVERTY

STUDIES ON THE EFFECTS OF SINGLE PARENTHOOD, THE FEMINIZATION OF POVERTY, AND HOMELESSNESS

edited by

STUART BRUCHEY
UNIVERSITY OF MAINE

A GARLAND SERIES

ELEMENTARY SCHOOL PRINCIPALS WHO CARE

RESPONDING TO SOCIAL CHANGE

CAROL M. HOFFMAN

GARLAND PUBLISHING, Inc.
NEW YORK & LONDON / 1997

Library of Congress Cataloging-in-Publication Data

Hoffman, Carol M.
    Elementary school principals who care : responding to social
change / Carol M. Hoffman.
        p.   cm. — (Children of poverty)
    Includes bibliographical references and index.
    ISBN 0-8153-2621-1 (alk. paper)
    1. Elementary school administration—Social aspects—United
States. 2. Elementary school principals—United States. 3. Social
change—United States. I. Title. II. Series.
LB2822.5.H64 1997
372.12'01—dc20
                                                    96-36695

Printed on acid-free, 250-year-life paper
Manufactured in the United States of America

To the memory of my Mother who, in spite of the negative effects of social change, grew up to be the most caring, responsible, intelligent and resourceful person I ever knew.

Contents

Tables

Introduction

As never before in the history of public education, public schools are under attack within their own communities. Yet, public schools are mirrors that allow communities to reflect themselves. For more than a decade, communities do not appear to like the reflection that bounces back to them. However, they tend to attack the mirror instead of the image that produces the reflection in the first place. They are confused between which one is the cause and which one is the effect. It's somewhat like the relationship between the messenger and the message. Human beings who make up communities and the larger society find it much easier to throw stones at the mirror or kill the messenger than to "fix" themselves.

Social change has spilled over into every community across the country. Public schools indeed mirror the negative effects of that social change.

The term *social change* means many things to many people. There is complexity and ambiguity to the term social change. On the other hand, the title and role of the elementary principal seem clearer and much easier to understand. There is more agreement among people as to what — and who — is an elementary principal. Attempting to marry a complex term (social change) with a simpler concept (elementary principal) proved to be a very difficult task. In the end, however, I discovered the *person* called the elementary principal was every bit as complex as the term to which he or she was being "married." I discovered a complex person was necessary in the role of elementary principal — at least in today's elementary school. Only a complex person in that role can respond effectively to the negative effects of social change as they impact his or her school. And so, the elementary principal became as complex as the term social change. The marriage of the two was (and is) a successful one!

Initially, I came up with a list of 26 social change *issues* impacting in negative ways on the elementary school and, ultimately, the elementary principal. Eventually, I whittled that list down to what appeared to be a more manageable twelve. In the end, however, even twelve social change issues were too many to bring into a formal study. After months of thinking and exploring how best to solve the dilemma of what to keep and what to discard, I decided to apply the Pandora's Box solution. I placed what I considered 12 essential social change issues in a box, put the lid on and shook that box with vim and vigor. Then I closed my eyes, lifted the lid and took out seven pieces of paper. Returning the lid to the box, I sat on the floor and read the words printed on those seven pieces of paper.

These are the words that "escaped" from Pandora's Box: poverty, single parent families, mothers in the workforce, child care, child abuse, cultural diversity and drug and alcohol abuse. At last I had my social change issues! It was time to begin the study in a formal sense.

Interviewing and analyzing data collected from elementary principals identified as responding in positive ways to the negative effects of social change was one of the most fascinating and meaningful experiences of my lifetime. Even a year later, I am awed by the work — indeed, the commitment and activation of caring — measured in each and every principal interviewed. If public education is to both survive and thrive, we might be able to credit elementary principals like those who appear in this book with saving what critics consider a sinking ship.

Public education can and must become something different, something better, something more relevant to the needs of children. Social change has drastically altered the needs of today's children. The impact of social change must be recognized by educators everywhere, although social change issues must never be used as excuses for public schools to lower the academic or behavioral standards of students.

Elementary principals appearing in this book offer great hope to the students and teachers in our public schools. If I live long enough, I might some day hear a child say, "My principal," when asked the question: Who is your hero?

Acknowledgements

To researchers and librarians in many parts of this country, most of whom I have never met face-to-face, I extend my thanks. Without their considerable knowledge and accommodating response to my frequent requests, I would have lacked the varied resources necessary to undertake my own study.

To Temple University's Dr. Robert Walter, Dr. Donald Walters and Dr. Catherine Soundy, my gratitude for their support and guidance.

To Dr. Stanley Dubelle for his mentorship during the research and analysis phase of the project.

To Dr. Stuart Bruchey and Mr. Michael Galligan, I extend my thanks for making this book possible.

To Mark "Wiz" Wisniewski, my deep appreciation for helping me with the computer software assistance I so badly needed. Mark's sobriquet, "Wiz," is quite appropriate.

Finally, my husband of 37 years deserves special thanks for sharing his wife with a Macintosh-SE for the last few years of our long marriage. Bruce has shown atypical patience during all phases of the research and book-writing process as well as his usual love and affection. Our three children, Jill, Ted, and Tod, our daughter-in-law, Denise, son-in-law, Jerry and our perfect granddaughters, Kristin and Morgan, remain most important to me.

For all of the above blessings, I am grateful.

Elementary School Principals Who Care

I

Social Change: The Impact

Ward and June Cleaver are dead. Dead, too, is their somewhat romanticized model of the traditional all-American family. Ward's and June's children, Beaver and Wally, are now middle-aged men, attempting to raise their own children in a society in which the traditional family has all but disintegrated.

Yearning for a return to the traditional family will not make it happen. Gone is gone. Something intervened between the traditional Cleaver family model idealized on television in the 1950s and the non-traditional family models of today. That "something" was social change, the combined, cumulative effects of increasingly complex social issues over a relatively short period of time.

The purpose of this book is to explore the negative effects of social change on the elementary school and to assist the elementary principal in responding in positive ways to those negative effects. Children are the prime beneficiaries of any school's efforts to make schooling more relevant to their present and future needs. Before we can begin to explore children's educational tomorrows, we must first understand their todays. What is it like to be two or four or six or eight or ten years old and growing up right now in the USA? Let's find out, beginning with what happened to children after the Cleaver family disappeared from the scene.

Rapid social change is what happened to America's children. While some children may have been helped by social change, many, many more have been hurt. Whether or not this hurt will create short-term or long-term damage to the developing person remains to be seen. Whatever the final outcome, social change *has* negatively impacted on children, families and public schools. This book is about what happened, how what happened affected the elementary school and what we can do about it. As such, this book is a slice of hard reality with a twist of hope through the caring action of school personnel. The elementary school person who

3

will be expected to actively lead and caringly respond to what happened is the elementary principal.

The pervasive, all-consuming nature of rapid social change over three decades appears to have no historical equal. In terms of structural consequences to our society, there's never been anything like it. Social change has created both positive and negative consequences for people and institutions. The focus of this book, however, is on the negative consequences to public schools, specifically the elementary school.

Social change is challenging public schools in many ways. Like a whirling dervish, the effects of social change have entered every classroom in the United States. As a result, educational leaders are discovering that within the traditional kindergarten through twelfth grade system, the curriculum now includes drug, alcohol and AIDS education, courses of study on coping and decision-making skills, self-esteem projects, nonviolent conflict resolution training, parenting courses and suicide, pregnancy and school drop-out prevention programs.

Public schools offer other non-traditional curricula and services such as breakfast, day care, after-school latch-key programs, special education for preschoolers with developmental problems, infant care programs for students who are also parents and full-day kindergarten for four and five years olds.

Today, social change has dramatically transformed the structure, focus and mission of traditional public schooling. As traditional schooling is being challenged through change, so, too, are school leaders.

Since public education is currently perceived as the logical solution to social problems it neither created nor coveted, school personnel are not necessarily welcoming these problems with open arms. Still, welcoming with open arms — or, at least, not barring children's entry— will be expected as more and more children appear at the schoolhouse door damaged or at least, adversely affected in physical, mental, or psychological ways by the negative effects of social change.

Change over time almost always has social implications. Social implications tend to be both bad and good, as well as ever-changing. Social change is a natural outgrowth of change over time.

Social change is nothing new. Why, then do so many people in our society see social change as some sort of aberration unique to the past thirty years? Perhaps it is the rapidity and complexity of contemporary social change that makes the *effects* of that change appear unique, as well as more negative than positive. Whatever the reasons, we must recognize the myriad effects of social change on public education. More important, public education must respond more effectively to the negative effects of social change as they impact on today's families, children and schools.

Change itself is neither positive nor negative. Instead, change is assigned positive and negative attributes through the perceptions of people affected by that particular change. *Social* change as it impacts on public schools, therefore, is perceived by principals, teachers and other school personnel affected by that change as either positive or negative. It is important for us to know how educational leaders perceive social change and what they are doing about it in their schools. One could safely suggest *most* educational leaders perceive social change as having a serious negative impact on children in our public schools.

Social *issues* can be called expressions — even consequences — of a society's needs, wants, values and behaviors. In order for us to recognize the impact of social change on this place called school, we must first recognize that social issues combined over a thirty year period to create present social change.

There is a cumulative effect to social issues. Social issues exist in abundance and are indeed impacting on children, their families, and ultimately, our public schools. Here is a sampling of major social issues.

A Dozen Social Issues
- Poverty
- Single parent families
- Mothers in the workforce
- Child care
- Child abuse
- Drug and alcohol abuse
- Cultural diversity
- Teen pregnancy
- Venereal diseases among students
- AIDS
- Violence in school
- Dropping out of school

The above list of a dozen is by no means complete but rather a synthesis of research on social issues. An analysis of the above incomplete list, however, would reveal that only one social issue is unique to the final decade of the 20th century: *AIDS*. All the other social issues on the list have existed as long as public education has been in existence.

If 11 of the 12 aforementioned social issues have been present ever since the first school bell rang, why, then, are today's public school personnel finding social issues difficult to deal with?

The answer to this question lies in the rapid growth and complexity of each *single* social issue and the *cumulative* effects of the problems arising from each social issue! Clearly, the cumulative effects have compounded to create the proverbial straw that is presently breaking the backs of both Uncle Sam *and* Ms. Liberty. Clearly, our public schools are in serious trouble as a result of the growth spurts of the negative effects of social change.

Even though public education has had years of "social issues" experience under its belt, public schools have never before been asked to accept and solve social problems compounded by the growth and complexity of single social issues.

To drive this point home, consider this: In times of slow social change, when society caught a cold, public schools sneezed. Since social change has become so complex and rapid, society's "cold" is now pneumonia. When society has pneumonia, public schools must receive antibiotics. Aspirin has been rendered ineffective.

If public education refuses antibiotics and decides, instead, to call upon past experiences for assistance in educating today's students, is there anything in the past to apply to the present and future? Are there enough educational aspirins and band-aids to go around, one more time? Will a completely new breed of elementary teachers and principals be required tomorrow or can yesterday's and today's teachers and principals learn to adapt to the demands of social change?

If the answers to the above questions do not seem obvious now, they will become obvious before the reader completes the final chapter.

SOCIAL ISSUES BECOME SOCIAL CHANGE

The concept of *social change* and the listing of all *social issues* as they apply to public education are too pervasive to explore well in a single book. With this in mind, let us select just seven of the twelve social issues listed earlier as our focus on social change. A definition of social change, therefore, will include those seven social issues.

Social change is an increase in poverty, single parent families, mothers in the workforce, child care, child abuse, drug and alcohol abuse and cultural diversity and their cumulative negative impact on children, the elementary school and the elementary principal.

Elementary teachers, counselors, librarians and other elementary staff members are first in line to do daily battle with children negatively affected by social change. Much has been written about ways to reach and teach students experiencing the negative effects of social change, for example, articles and books on classroom management, teaching/learning styles, cooperative learning and other strategies to use during the teaching-learning process. Little has been written, however, for and about the embattled elementary principal and his or her own struggle with school leadership and social change.

There are at least four reasons to concentrate on students in the elementary school as well as the elementary principal.

1. The elementary school is the first level of public education to feel and experience the effects of rapid and complex social change. Earlier response to the negative effects of social change, therefore, offers more hope for children as learners and achievers.

2. *Prevention of numerous learning problems* associated with the negative effects of social change is more likely to occur in the elementary school than in the secondary school.

3. *When outright prevention of learning problems* is unlikely or even impossible, remediation and other intervention strategies are best begun in the elementary school.

4. The elementary principal, as instructional leader of the school as well as manager of daily operations, will be expected to find effective ways to "solve" school problems associated with social change.

Today's elementary principal is just emerging from a state of shock regarding the cumulative effects of social change on the elementary school. Traditional "ed leadership" preparation rarely is in sync with the needs of today's and tomorrow's elementary school principals. It is probably true in all 50 states that whenever a new elementary principal position is advertised, an elementary principal rooted in traditional educational perception and skills need not apply. A scientific study would almost surely validate what educators in the field already know: the impact of social change is requiring principal attitudes and behaviors quite different from principal attitudes and behaviors of the past. What used to work well for elementary principals works no longer.

Public education tends to be slow to respond effectively to the needs of today's elementary student. Old ways are like a security blanket. We may have outgrown the need for the blanket but we cling to it anyway because it feels right and is awfully comforting during times of stressful change.

Traditional elementary principals began to sense and feel the stress of social change thirty years ago, first with Head Start, followed quickly by an increase in mothers in the workforce and the birth of the day care movement. For most of those thirty years, the traditional elementary principal attempted to resist the force of change until he could resist no longer. One traditional elementary principal recently responded to social change by retiring. This principal told colleagues, "When I saw a four-year old walking the halls of my school, I knew it was time for me to quit. In no way should public schools be accepting children under five years of age! If women stayed home where they belong and fathers worked and didn't abandon their children, there would be no need for this ridiculous idea called 'early intervention.'"

This principal is not alone among today's elementary principals in attitude and behavior regarding social change as it impacts on today's elementary school.

Let's look now at the retired principal's reference, this idea called "early intervention," an idea that will not go away soon, if ever. While early intervention programs in public schools logically offer the most hope of all for preschoolers damaged in some way by the negative effects of social change, the majority of preschoolers in this country will not likely participate in these programs. There are several reasons for this, the main one being the lack of opportunity due to lack of supportive funding. What must be made perfectly clear to elementary principals and their school personnel is the likelihood that most social-issues-damaged preschoolers will enter public kindergarten without having experienced an early intervention program.

The largest and best-known early intervention program is Head Start. Head Start is a federally funded program that enrolls 647,273 preschoolers but, in fact, enrolls fewer than 20% of the children eligible for the program. [1] Lack of funding is the reason why more than 80% of this nation's poorest, experiences-impoverished children will enter public kindergarten without having been in a Head Start program, even though they are eligible for this program. The federal government is being criticized not only for failing to address the social conditions that weakened a family's ability to support its children but also for retreating from its earlier commitment to poor families.

Poverty is the social issue most damaging to children, families, and ultimately, the public school. Childhood poverty statistics are alarming. Among industrialized countries, the United States has the highest childhood poverty rate, often two to three times higher than the others. One-third of America's students are considered poor. National trends are frightening. The earliest poverty data came in 1969 when the poverty rate was 15.3%. Today, the poverty rate for children under the age of six has increased 67.3% since 1969.[2]

While *poverty* is seen as the most serious issue facing children, families and public schools, other social issues prevail. For example, *Women in the Workforce* remains an important issue as the mothers of more than 10 million preschoolers now need child care. The number of mothers in the workforce will continue to grow, especially among single mothers. However, the majority of married women with children under six are already in the labor force[3].

More and more children appear to be not ready to enter the classroom and succeed in this place called school. Are the elementary schools, in turn, not ready for the children? Is it possible that elementary schools may never truly be "ready" to meet the needs of all social-issues-damaged students? Can school principals become ready to lead teachers, counselors, librarians, paraprofessionals and service personnel in meeting children's needs? Do elementary principals truly know what it means when more than two-thirds of their new kindergartners have already been in away-from-home learning environments connected with child care? Does the elementary principal truly grasp the implications for his or her role as educational leader of the elementary school? Does the elementary principal have any idea how different entering kindergarten was for Beaver and Wally Cleaver than it will be for Carrie, Chad, Marci and Felipe?

Carrie

Five mornings a week, Carrie has no memory of being lifted from her bed just before sun-up and carried to the car. She has no memory of being lifted from the car seat, carried to the day care center and transferred to the waiting arms of the day care aide who then transfers her to a bean bag chair for two more hours of sleep.

Each Monday through Friday, at approximately 8:30 am, Carrie awakens in a bean bag chair ten miles from home. Her sleepy eyes always search frantically for the smiling face of Anna, her favorite day care person. Carrie's greatest fear is that Anna will soon leave her just as all her other smiling day care people left — without saying "goodbye." It isn't easy to keep adjusting to adults moving in and out of your life, especially those who smile.

Carrie is four years old. In her short lifetime, she has had to adjust to her mother's frequent moves in and out of her life. She has also had to adjust to frequent moves in and out of her maternal grandmother's house, the house that belongs to the grandmother who never smiles. Carrie seems to live in a world of women who rarely or never smile. Men are almost unknown to her. Whenever Carrie sees a father or grandfather come to the center to pick up a child, she is curious. She has never seen her father or grandfather and, although she doesn't know it yet, she never will.

Carrie is among the growing majority of preschool age children in the United States: children not yet age-eligible for kindergarten, enrolled in a day care center from 6:30 am to 5:30 pm, living with a single mother who works fulltime at a low-paying job. Occasionally, when the bills consume Carrie's mother, she needs to shuffle her child care arrangement to an unsmiling, unpaid grandma for days or weeks.

Since Carrie presently lives with her mother who sometimes has enough energy to smile and who appears to love her, people say she is one of the lucky ones. We will visit Carrie in 20 years for . . . the rest of the story.

Chad

Chad is not allowed to enroll in Carrie's day care center because he still wets his pants. Children who have reached their third birthday are forbidden to wet or soil their pants. Chad is four, one year over the wet-pants cut-off. Last month he was given a trial run but he and his bladder blew it within two days. One "accident" is allowed in this center but when the second "accident" occurs, the kid's out.

Chad's father is furious about his son's failure to meet the major criterion for day care enrollment. He is even more furious because now he has to drive Chad to an Aunt's house, an extra 20 miles each day. All the way to and from the Aunt's house, Chad has to deal with his father's angry words and gestures. Whenever Chad draws into himself in order to screen out the yelling and arm-waving, his father reaches over and smacks him. Sometimes he hits Chad in the face or across his left ear. Mostly, however, he hits Chad where no one can see the results.

Chad's father has had five different jobs this year. His present job pays two dollars over minimum hourly wage. Alcohol abuse tends to get in the way of stable employment and a decent salary. Being a single parent adds to life's frustrations and anxieties. Chad's father is one of a growing number of men raising their child or children without a mother in the home. Still, people say Chad is one of the lucky ones because at least he has a father and most of his little friends don't. We will visit Chad in 20 years to find out if he truly was one of the lucky ones.

Marci

Marci is another four-year old who goes to day care Monday through Friday. Marci's mother and father enjoy a combined income of six figures, so they can afford a high quality child care program. Marci's parents can also afford a sitter to come into the home evenings. When two parents work at all-consuming careers, evening meetings are common. As a result, the sitter frequently picks up Marci from the day care center and drives her home, feeds her supper, watches television with her and then puts her to bed.

Marci's favorite day is Saturday. This is breakfast day with Mom and Dad. Sunday, however, is Marci's un-favorite day. She's never sure where she'll be spending Sunday, although she is sure it won't be with her mother and father. It seems Mom and Dad need Sunday for social time with their friends.

People say Marci is definitely one of the lucky ones. She is the four-year old daughter of a mother and father who happen to love her as well as each other. Marci is, therefore, a member of an "intact" family. She will never want for anything material, as her parents are financially well-off. What she wants, however, costs nothing in dollars and cents: her parents' time. In the course of a seven-day week the actual hours Marci's parents spend with her can be counted on one hand. Some weeks, two fingers are left over after the count. Within twenty years, we will know if Marci truly was one of the lucky ones.

Felipe

Felipe spends almost 60 hours a week in the day care center. He knows every square inch of that 20' x 18' room. Felipe's mother and father are presently employed at minimum-wage jobs, although each experiences periods of unemployment, whenever fruit and vegetable picking opportunities are scarce. At present, Felipe's father is at home recuperating from a work-related injury. The father's injury is a minor one that would allow him to care for Felipe at home, but he chooses to deliver Felipe to day care at 6 am every week day.

The child care workers resent Felipe's father's unwillingness to care for his son at home whenever he or his wife is not working. The child care workers resent the other parents who are receiving ADF (Aid to Dependent Families) assistance, yet appear to be abusing the system. Felipe's parents pay only a nominal weekly fee for child care — $4.50. The bulk of their child care fees — $76.50 — are government-subsidized.

Felipe is a sensitive four year old who feels the resentment of those who care for him 60 hours a week. He tries to be good and stay out of everybody's way but with 22 other preschoolers in a 20' x 18' room, he finds himself in the time-out chair at least a hundred times a day. Or so it seems, to a four-year old boy named Felipe. While people do not see Felipe as one of the lucky ones, they tend to resent him as a welfare child. Within twenty years we will know how these perceptions and attitudes impacted on Felipe.

The family life structure of the above examples of four-year olds combined is representative of the family life structure of most four year olds living in the United States. The above examples combined paint a word-picture of daily life for the vast majority of preschoolers living in this country. Child care needs are the common denominator, no matter in which family array four-year olds and other preschoolers find themselves. The most common family arrays are children living with one parent, two parents, one parent and one step-parent, one parent and that parent's boyfriend/girlfriend, grandparents, foster care or other relatives or guardians.

The need for child care other than parent care is now a need for two-thirds of this nation's preschoolers. The need for before and after school child care for school age children is even greater.

Next school year, Carrie, Chad, Marci and Felipe will enter public kindergarten. Will public kindergarten — indeed, public *education* — be ready to accept and meet the varied and complex needs of these young children, needs that go far beyond learning to read, write and compute?

Who will provide effective help to our kindergarten, first grade and other elementary teachers whose students are affected in negative ways by social change? In the elementary school, first in line to help teachers, librarians, counselors, nurses, and other staff members is the elementary principal. Over the next decade, the leadership role of the elementary school principal will be challenged as never before.

A serious look at today's elementary principal and his or her response to the negative effects of social change seems long overdue. This book attempts to take that serious look.

Carrie, Chad, Marci and Felipe are depending on it.

ELEMENTARY PRINCIPALS WHO CARE

We met four preschoolers soon headed for public school Kindergarten. Let's now meet two Elementary Principals that Carrie, Chad, Marci and Felipe may be lucky enough to call their own.

Martin and Meredith care enough to attempt to walk — even run — that two-lane path that leads to becoming more responsive, effective principals. Meredith is *an* elementary principal in a large city in Pennsylvania. She has been a principal for 18 years. Martin is *the* elementary principal of a rural school in Texas which has recently been affected in negative ways by rapid social change. He has been a principal for almost 25 years. Both elementary principals wish to remain anonymous, although both agreed to share some of their daily experiences.

Martin

Martin reaches for the tie he removed after his fourth crisis of the morning. By the time the final bell rings and the last kid leaves the school, Martin has racked up no fewer than twenty-one crises. It is now 6:15 pm. In another forty-five minutes, Martin will be speaking to the Home-School Association about badly needed playground equipment and badly needed parent volunteers. Afterwards, he will rush to the Board of Education meeting in order to plead his case regarding budget cuts. If Martin is lucky, he'll get home by eleven, grab a sandwich and a diet Pepsi, open his mail, read an educational article he's been trying to read for weeks and collapse in bed about midnight.

As Martin adjusts his collar, smooths his shirt-front and attempts to look more "professional," he is struck with how "unprofessional" he feels. Since all the people in the school have gone home for the day, Martin expresses his "unprofessional" feelings to himself. In a five-minute monologue, Martin tells himself what it's really like to be an educational leader in a growing number of public schools in rural America.

He begins with his first crisis, Mrs. Clark's substitute teacher, who quit after the Pledge to the Flag. Just like that, she buzzed Martin's office and said she doesn't have to put up with children who not only don't want to learn but who also show no respect for teachers and the American flag. Then she walked out.

Two minutes later, Martin rushed in.

He spent the next twenty minutes reading a book to fifth graders who *do* frequently show no respect for teachers and the flag — principals, too. When a hardier substitute teacher for Mrs. Clark showed up, Martin flew to his second crisis, a first grade terror whose habitual use of the F-word was too much for the high-strung music teacher.

By the time Martin recalls his tenth crisis of the day, it is time for the Home-School Association meeting. Somehow, Martin never finds enough time to enjoy what he believes would be a theraputic experience — describing *all* the crises on his daily crisis list to someone, anyone, even his office walls.

Martin is a typical elementary principal — overworked, underappreciated and undervalued. If Martin had time to figure out his true hourly rate he would discover his hourly rate is just a few cents over minimum wage. Just like so many of his colleagues, Martin did not choose his profession for the paycheck. The paycheck was secondary to his love for kids and the teaching-learning process. He used to love his work and now wonders where that love has gone. It's not that he hates his work, it's just that he doesn't feel the excitement his work used to generate *every single day. Every single day!*

These days, instead of feeling motivated every single day, Martin tends to feel discouraged and enervated. Some weeks it's difficult for him to identify just one good minute, a minute in which he felt he had made a difference for today's kids and their teachers. When Martin's thoughts become reflective, he realizes he can't remember when he experienced one good solid day as an educational leader— at least over the last five years. He almost believes his rural school has become urbanized, right before his eyes! As a result, Martin now sees himself more of a combination policeman, fireman, psychologist and social worker than an educational leader. Martin worries about the present and future of public education as well as his place in it.

Martin cares.

Martin cares enough to hug an eight year old who needs a hug even though some of his colleagues warn him against touching a student, even for comfort or to show paternal affection. Martin cares enough to support an after-school child care center in the school's gym, even though the community's senior citizens are vehemently against such a center because they suspect taxpayer dollars are supporting it. Martin cares enough to beg the parents of his students to take a free evening parenting course sponsored by the school, even though less than 3% of the parents attend the course.

Martin cares enough to move against the tide by breaking away from the tenets of traditional schooling and traditional school leadership.

There are dozens of social-driven problems Martin and other "rural" elementary school principals are wrestling with right now. If you find this hard to believe, contact Martin or your own rural or neighborhood principal.

Meredith

In the principal's tiny office on an almost typical Thursday, Meredith smooths her wrinkled skirt. Actually, her skirt is more than wrinkled. At noon, her skirt was attacked by the teeth of Jaws, a Pit Bull brought to the first grade pet show. Although Jaws did not win a prize as biggest, prettiest or best-behaved pet, he nonetheless stole the show. Some of the first graders wanted to award Jaws a prize for worst-behaved pet but that prize category had not been established and, besides, Meredith wanted to minimize Jaw's very existence.

The first graders watching Jaws hang onto to the principal's skirt hem for dear life either shrieked in terror or howled with laughter. Meredith attempted to show no fear during the skirt "attack" but she suspected she was not entirely successful. While Meredith's experience with Jaws was not the only nor the worst experience that day, she nonetheless reflected on that particular incident for a long time.

Once Meredith pieced together all the Jaws information fed her by children, parents and teachers, she sank into the emotional pits (no pun intended). The pieces of information Meredith put together produced a disturbing picture. While Janine was the first grader who "brought" Jaws to the pet show, Janine was not his owner. It seems Jaws was owned by Janine's mother's current boyfriend, a 17 year old named Nuke. Since Nuke now lives with Janine and her mother, he thought it would be funny for Janine to take his Pit Bull to the pet show. The main reason Nuke suggested Janine take Jaws was not because he cares about Janine and her schooling but rather because he has a pathological hatred for schools and everyone in them.

Nuke knew in advance that Jaws would attack someone. That's all he needed to know. The fact that Jaws attacked the school principal brought special delight to Nuke.

Meredith remembers Nuke as a discouraged school dropout who today actually believes his teachers and his schools "did him wrong" when he was a student, not so very long ago. He delights in hurting anyone and anything connected with that place called school. This time Nuke's delight came at Meredith's expense. Through Jaws, Nuke was able to pay back the educational system he felt had failed him. While Nuke's beliefs may be rooted in perceptive distortions and faulty logic, his beliefs, nevertheless, are all that matter to him. And he must and will act on those beliefs.

There are countless Nukes out there in our world just waiting to pay back some segment of society for perceived wrongs and injustices that society supposedly inflicted. The segment of society Nuke perceives "wronged" him is public education.

Meredith realizes she is beginning to encounter more and more parents and pretend parents who resemble Nuke in attitude, lifestyle and inappropriate, often hurtful behavior. She is wondering how many of these parents feel public education failed to meet their needs when they were students.

Meredith, like her colleague Martin, burns the midnight oil every school night. Also, like Martin, she often goes to school on Saturdays. The Saturday following her experience with Jaws, Meredith sat in her office wishing she could let herself cry, scream, or kick something. Early in her career, however, Meredith discovered she could not— would not — allow anyone to observe behaviors in her typically attributed to females in leadership roles. Tough, caring, bright and dedicated to educational excellence became the only kinds of descriptors Meredith would accept of herself. She was determined "never to let them see me sweat." whoever "them" happened to be. As a result, people observed only what Meredith wanted them to observe — a tough, caring, bright, high-standards elementary principal who also happened to be a woman. Now, on this Saturday morning in her undersized office, Meredith felt her image and resolve beginning to crumble. What was happening, she was certain, was a weakening of her inability to handle the mounting problems associated with social change.

Yet, in the final analysis, Meredith's greatest concern is with the children and their families. What will happen to them if she and other educational leaders fail?

As Meredith swivels her faded blue chair in the undersized office of River Street Elementary School, her thoughts abruptly brighten. She suddenly realizes how relieved she feels that Jaws attacked her and not one of the first graders. On a Saturday morning in Spring, Meredith discovers something that makes her smile. She is grateful that a Pet Show Pit Bull chose her instead of a child.

Meredith cares.

Meredith cares enough to make sure orange juice and granola bars are on hand for the growing number of students coming to school without breakfast, even though her Board of Education opposes applying for a government breakfast program. Meredith knows if she can't win the battle one way she'll search for new ammunition via PTA support. Meredith cares enough to remember to duck the slings and arrows aimed in her direction by more traditional principal colleagues. Her colleagues tell her she is making them look bad with her responses to social problems. They are angry with Meredith.

Meredith cares enough not to care what her colleagues think or say. This realization makes her laugh.

Of course, Meredith's thoughts turn serious as quickly as they had lightened. As she sits in her fading blue desk chair that Saturday morning, she realizes her role as educational leader of River Street Elementary School is becoming something else. Her professors at the university had never included courses — indeed nary a word — about social change and its impact on the elementary school and the school principal.

Are Martin and Meredith among few or many elementary principals demonstrating they care enough to respond in positive ways to the negative effects of social change? It may be impossible to measure the quality of caring and the activity of responding among today's elementary principals. Nevertheless, caring and responding will be required of tomorrow's elementary principals.

One question is answerable: Are today's elementary principals feeling the effects of social change as they impact on their elementary school? Most certainly, the answer is, "yes."

Elementary Principals everywhere are discovering how concerned they are with the impact of social change on public education. They are also discovering exhausting and sometimes frightening "principal" responsibilities that were never part of their original job description. Most certainly, the effects of social change are challenging every elementary principal whether that principal works in an urban, suburban or rural school. The needs and challenges of today's children, especially the youngest in our elementary schools, are forcing a new face on the old face of traditional schooling. Like it or not, ready or not, the effects of social change are already embedded in the fabric of the elementary school, Everywhere, U.S.A.

What is this phenomenon called "social change?" What does it really mean for both students and principals in our public elementary schools? Are caring principals like Martin and Meredith a dying breed, lovely aberrations found in very few places across this country? If there are other Martins and Merediths "out there," where are they and what are they doing to respond to the social change needs of children, staff and parents?

These questions and more have begged and nagged for many years. The time has come to answer — or at least attempt to answer them — through a formal study conducted by the author.

II

The Study Begins

People who fiercely resist change fail to understand that change itself is neither positive nor negative. Instead, change is assigned positive and/or negative attributes through the perceptions of people affected by change. Social change as it impacts on elementary schools, therefore, is perceived by principals, teachers and other school personnel affected by that change as either positive or negative. As stated earlier, this study will concentrate on perceived negative effects of social change on the elementary school.

In general, the traditional curriculum for the elementary grades has been found to be woefully inadequate in meeting the needs of children affected by social change. In particular, the primary grades are at the center of a strong movement headed by education leaders at the national level which would bring about immediate and innovative structural and curricular change. Early childhood organizations and influential political and civic leaders are vigorously demanding public schools become more responsive to the needs of this nation's youngest children. Early childhood advocates are demanding more state and federal dollars to assist families in need. The frightening thing about all of these good intentions is that home and school experiences appear to be more developmentally inappropriate than ever for our youngest children.

As a population, this nation's "youngest" are now identified as the population most negatively affected by social change, and more at risk of failure in school. Early childhood education outside the home no longer begins when children are five years of age, the typical entrance age for kindergarten. As a result of social change, new, non-traditional early childhood programs are now, and will continue, finding their way to public schools where they will join the ones already established. Preschool programs like Head Start, infant stimulation, day care, nursery school and kindergarten for three and four year olds will continue expanding

19

into public schools, requiring competent, visionary leadership along with the changing kindergarten through third grade curriculum.

The primary grades, however, do not stand alone as challenges to the elementary principal whose scope of responsibilities may extend as far as the sixth, seventh or eighth grade. Regardless of the elementary school grade level structure, the principal is the leader of social change as it affects the school's children, teachers, support staff and parents. In order to demonstrate the connection between the effects of social change and their challenge to the elementary principal, the author developed a series of premises. These premises take a circuitous route. They are listed in sequential order:

- Change is inevitable
- Social change is impacting not only on the developmental needs of today's children but also on the traditional structure, focus and mission of the public education system
- The education system as it exists today at the elementary level must change in structure, focus and mission in order to respond effectively to social change which includes change within the structure of the family
- Social change is impacting on elementary schools in both positive and negative ways. The negative impact will continue to challenge schools well into the twenty-first century
- The elementary principal must become more responsive to the negative effects of social change as they impact on children, teachers and parents because social change is woven into the fabric of our public schools
- Social change is, well, CHANGE!
- Change is inevitable

PURPOSE OF THE STUDY

The purpose of the study was to identify activities and characteristics of principals who are responding to the negative effects of social change as they impact on the elementary school.

SOCIAL ISSUES

As stated earlier, the author focused on seven major social change issues to which the elementary principal was responding through programs, procedures and staff development:

- poverty
- single parent families
- mothers in the workforce
- child care
- child abuse
- cultural diversity
- drug and alcohol abuse

The elementary principal was not expected to be addressing equally all social change issues. The principal, however, *was* expected to be addressing most social issues and perceiving all of them as important to address.

RESEARCH QUESTIONS

1. What is the elementary principal doing, through programs, procedures and staff development, to respond to the negative effects of social change as they impact on the elementary school?

2. Are there similarities between the principal's present school and his or her childhood school?

3. Are there similarities in the family structure of the principal and his or her students? Family structure includes socio-economic status, mother-father relationship, number of siblings and birth order positioning.

4. Who will the principal remember as people who were/are caring individuals?

5. Is there a characteristic-type pattern in the elementary principal who is responding to the negative effects of social change?

6. What is the gender, age, and experiential background of the principal who is responding to social change?

7. What is the basis for the principal's response to social change as it impacts on the school?

LIMITATIONS

The most recent data available through Pennsylvania's Department of Education revealed a population of 1,635 elementary principals. From that large population, a small population was selected. Principals selected were presently employed as elementary principals in three contiguous counties in south-eastern Pennsylvania. All three counties have similar socio-economic factors and similar numbers of elementary principals.

The author identified seven major social change issues impacting in negative ways on children and, inevitably, the elementary school: poverty, single parent families, mothers in the workforce, child care, child abuse, cultural diversity, and drug and alcohol abuse. While other major social change issues exist, for example AIDS and the homeless, the researcher chose to limit the study to seven issues. In reality, all social change issues are interrelated, making their effects difficult to study in isolation.

From a potential population of twelve principals, a population of ten emerged. With a population of ten, the findings cannot be generalized. The findings, therefore, will be confined to ten public school elementary principals recognized for their response to social change as it impacts on the elementary school.

DEFINITIONS

There are fifteen terms to define:

principal — the public school administrator who is state-certified and presently functioning as an elementary principal in Pennsylvania

elementary school — the place where a public school district's youngest students, usually kindergarten through sixth grade, are educated before entering the secondary school

activities — the work supported, undertaken or performed by the principal in response to social change

characteristics — an individual's distinguishing qualities or traits

responding — the positive ways in which the principal is addressing the negative effects of social change as they impact on the school. Responding implies the activation of caring

social change — an increase in the following: poverty, single parent families, mothers in the workforce, child care, child abuse, cultural diversity and drug and alcohol abuse which frequently impact in negative ways on children and schools

urban — a type of school located in a city where population density is great and where walking distance to school is relatively short

suburban — a type of school located just outside a city where population is less dense and where many students are bus students

rural — a type of school located a distance from a city where population is widely scattered and almost all students are bus students

lower class — a family's socio-economic status, perceived by the elementary principal as poor or needy

middle class — a family's socio-economic status, perceived by the elementary principal as neither rich nor poor

upper class — a family's socio-economic status, perceived by the elementary principal as rich or well-to-do

programs — curricula, activities and events implemented in the elementary school as a response to social change. The formal definition of program is, "A plan or procedure"[4]

procedures — the school's operational practices and guidelines implemented as responses to social change. The formal definition of procedure is, "The sequence of steps to be followed; a particular course of action."[5]

staff development — any activity or function intended to improve the school performance of teachers and other school personnel. According to Sergiovanni and Starratt, staff development is defined as ". . . part of the school's daily routine emphasis on personal and professional improvement."[6]

NEED FOR THE STUDY

Since public education is currently perceived by the general public as the logical solution to social problems it neither created nor coveted, school leaders are not necessarily welcoming these problems with open arms. Still, "welcoming with open arms" will be expected as more and more young children appear at the schoohouse door damaged or at least adversely affected in physical, mental, or psychological ways by the negative effects of rapid social change.

Critics of public education are both vocal and bountiful. Here is one recent example. The cover of the April 1995 edition of the popular *Phi Delta Kappan* depicts public education as a sinking ship — more specifically, the Titanic on its way down. The author of the feature article is quoted on the cover as saying, "Let's declare education a disaster and get on with our lives."[7]

On the other hand, critics of public schools also cling to the belief that public schools are capable of meeting the challenges of social change in order to make our nation better in every way. A recent publication compiled by the Center on National Education Policy has a catchy title: *Do We Still Need Public Schools?* By the time the reader finishes reading the booklet, the answer to the question is obvious. Yes, of course, we still need public schools. At least the authors lead the reader to this conclusion![8]

The elementary principal will inevitably be expected to perform as the leader who seeks solutions to social problems invading the elementary school. The principal may be lacking in basic knowledge about social change as well as essential caring about the effects of social change. The principal's attitude about social change may be in conflict with the needs of children negatively affected by social change. Few, if any, practical long-range plans exist for the successful integration of social-driven programs, procedures and staff development in the public schools. Since the elementary principal is the leader of programs, procedures and staff development in the elementary school, it is essential to help the principal prepare for the challenge of social change. One way to help the principal prepare for the challenge might be to identify principals already responding in positive ways to the negative effects of social change.

More than ever before, the elementary principal must be a caring person. Author Nel Noddings postulates there is a "crisis of caring" in our schools.[9] Noddings writes, "The primary aim of every educational institution and of every educational effort must be the maintenance and enhancement of caring.[10] In order to clarify any misconception about the aim of education, Noddings postulates further. She writes that while schools must not abdicate their primary responsibility to enhance the intellect, schools must not put the ideal of caring at risk.[11] The principal who is responding to social change is a principal who is not putting the ideal of caring at risk.

Studies that attempt to identify the socially responsive principal or characteristics of a socially responsive principal could not be located in a review of the literature. The concept of the principal as a leader who must deal with social change may be an idea whose time is just now arriving.

A well-known spokesman for public education reminds educators that the traditional model of schooling, inspired by the factory, is dead. He encourages educational leaders to abandon the traditional model of schooling because clinging to it will mean total disaster.[12]

The task at hand for elementary principals everywhere is a most difficult one if a positive response to the negative effects of social change is to occur. A positive response must, in fact, occur if the elementary school is to meet the complex needs of today's student caught in the middle of rapid social change.

III

What Does the Literature Have to Say?

A review of the literature revealed an abundance of related topics but no single study that assimilated, synthesized and evaluated this problem. The negative effects of social change on children, however, are already well-documented. We will now examine more fully the social issues that create the social change impacting on the elementary schools and, ultimately, the elementary principal.

SOCIAL ISSUES

Impact on Children and Families

Recent demographic studies revealed the following statistics:

More than one in five American children — 15 million — lives in poverty.[13] This nation's official poverty figure for the year 1995 was $14,763, for a family of four.[14]

This is what is happening with children each day in America:

- 2,699 babies are born into poverty
- 3 children die from child abuse
- 100,000 are homeless
- 1,200,000 children arrive home from school, unsupervised, to a house where there is a gun[15]

Additional statistics, compiled by UNICEF, are equally discouraging. World-wide, the mortality rate for children under five years of age was studied in 145 countries. The United States ranks 121st. In order to make sense of a ranking of 121, a comparison with other nations is necessary. Cuba, for example, ranked 120th, just one below the U.S., while the Czech Republic ranked 122nd, one ahead of the U.S. Japan ranked 142nd while the safest country in which to survive the preschool years was Finland, which ranked 145th.[16]

Child care will continue to be a pressing issue. At present, four out of five children in school will have mothers in need of before and after-school child care. Two-thirds of all preschoolers will have mothers in the workforce who are in need of child care. The government assistance waiting list for child care continues to grow and grow. In New Jersey, 14,000 children are on a waiting list for child care assistance. The list in Texas is almost 36,000 and in Georgia, 41,000.[17]

A review of the literature uncovered no systematic study of the principal's perceptions or attitudes toward social change issues that are bringing children to school in need of child care. One survey sought the principal's opinion of establishing child care programs in public schools. This survey, however, never mentioned the principal's feelings about day care nor implied the principal's role in day care programs that will inevitably expand into public schools.[18]

Child care is just one major social issue impacting on today's elementary schools. The use and abuse of alcohol and other drugs is another.

Today's children are directly exposed to drugs and alcohol long before they reach adolescence. The use of illegal drugs is becoming prevalent among elementary students. A Study a few years ago indicated drug use among sixth graders had tripled over the last ten years.[19] One of the latest statistics available is an attention-getter. Within the last month, almost 23% of students as young as 11 and 12 were solicited to buy drugs.[20] Almost 12% of junior high students reported they drank beer during the last few weeks while almost 6% reported they smoked marijuana during that same time period.[21]

The alarming increase of drug damage to children before they are born is well-documented. Drug-damaged children are now entering public schools displaying an array of learning and behavior problems. Fetal alcohol syndrome and cocaine addiction in the womb can mean permanent damage to the brain and body of a newborn. There is no way to predict what learning and behavioral problems drug and alcohol-damaged babies will be bringing to school. Since the systematic study of drug and alcohol-damaged babies has just begun, the oldest children being studied are just now entering kindergarten. Public schools, therefore, are still a year or two away from finding out what kinds of learning and behavioral problems those drug and alcohol-damaged kindergartners will bring to the classroom.

The Children's Defense Fund provides statistics that show an alarming increase in child abuse since 1982. Death is often the outcome of child abuse, to which the Children's Defense Fund says, "The deaths of children from child abuse and neglect are a tragic reminder that our nation is guilty of public neglect. [22]

An authority on child abuse, particularly in the areas of incest and sexual abuse, addressed Berks County (PA) medical personnel and counselors a number of years ago in a two-hour seminar. His statistics included the following:

The number of countable, verifiable sexually abused children tripled between 1980 and 1986.

25% of the adults who sexually abuse children are their parents.

51% of children who are physically abused were also sexually abused.

85% of the adults who sexually abuse children are known and trusted by the children they abuse.

Only 15% of child abusers are strangers.

The average length of time from onset to disclosure of sexual abuse is 3.8 years.[23] More recent studies indicate there were more than a million child abuse cases confirmed in 1993, although three million were actually reported. Of those confirmed, the forms of child abuse fell into two major categories: neglect was 50% while physical abuse was 36%.[24]

Today's family structure is changing more rapidly than data can accurately reflect. The disruption of changing family structure often contributes to the problems children are bringing to school.

The single parent population is on the rise as the social stigma once associated with divorce or giving birth out of wedlock has lifted. Studies indicate, however, that a single mother of just one child cannot escape poverty, when working fulltime at a minimum wage job. Poverty is always more prevalent for children living with a single mother. For example, 50% of children living with mother alone were poor compared with 12% who lived with both parents.[25] The Aid to Dependent Families with Children (ADFC) and food stamp benefits to single parents increase every year. Alabama ranks first while Alaska ranks last.[26] A high risk profile has been compiled by the FBI. Included on that high risk profile are children living in a single parent family. A study indicated 70% of children ages four to nine arrested for a serious crime lived with a single parent.[27]

Cultural diversity is also bringing social-related changes to school. Public schools in America are growing in cultural diversity. Today, 33% of urban students are African-American while 22% are Hispanic.[28] However, the Hispanic population is increasing at a faster rate than the African-American population. A recent government demographic study indicates there is a Latino-izing of America. Currently there are 27 million Latinos in the U.S. That number is expected to increase to 88 million by the middle of the 21st century.[29] Cultural diversity is not impacting solely on public schools in states bordering Mexico. For example, school districts in Montgomery County, Maryland, are receiving 3,000 new students a year, mostly immigrants from Vietnam, El Salvador, Nicaragua and the former Soviet Union. A somewhat humorous side effect is that with so many students to feed, the first lunch line begins at 10 am![30]

Impact on Schools and Principals

The educational needs of this nation's elementary school children will challenge the elementary principal in many ways. The principal will be involved more and more with social issues that will impact on the curriculum. One researcher suggests today's school curriculum is ". . .at odds with the experiences, backgrounds, hopes and wishes of many students."[31] The elementary school will change in kinds of services provided as the effects of social change bring younger children into public education. Accepting children younger than the traditional kindergarten age will soon become commonplace in the elementary school. The elementary principal will need to gain new knowledge about how young children learn. The negative effects of child abuse and fetal drug and alcohol use will almost surely include children's capacity for "school learning." A child's environment most certainly influences intelligence and the capacity to succeed in school. It is widely known that even small amounts of prenatal alcohol have damaging effects on the developing fetus.[32]

Findings in a recent Clark Foundation study are not encouraging. Principal development appears to be almost nonexistent, even for those expected to lead reform in difficult situations.[33]

In the poverty and drug-ridden Ghetto of the Bronx, author Jonathan Kozol asks resident Mrs. Washington, "Do you think America likes children?" Mrs. Washington's reply is, "I don't think so."[34]

Can how much elementary principals "like" children — in other words, care about them — make the difference between children's failure in school and their success? There is great hope that today's and tomorrow's elementary principals will care very much about all the children in their schools.

TODAY'S ELEMENTARY PRINCIPAL

Needs, Practices, Policies

The elementary principal is seen as lacking in basic knowledge in the areas of child development and learning theory. In a study a few years ago, this premise surfaced when half the principals surveyed expressed support for terminating the administration of paper-pencil tests in the primary grades. These principals believed such practice has harmful effects on young students. These same principals, however, revealed they feel pressured to produce higher test scores and that test scores indeed determine what is taught in primary classrooms.[35] As a result, the elementary principal continues to support practices he or she believes to be developmentally inappropriate. Studies abound which find potential school dropouts tend to live in this nation's lowest socioeconomic "underclass."[36] The elementary principal must understand that, by third grade, more than 70% of all potential dropouts can be identified. Developmentally appropriate early intervention strategies and programs, therefore, must become familiar to elementary principals whose youngest students are adversely affected by social change.[37]

The elementary principal of a school where social change is rapid and cultural diversity is common would benefit from understanding the work of Erik Erikson. The focus of Erikson's model of psychosocial development " . . . is on the maturing person as the person experiences new sociocultural spheres and roles."[38] Most certainly, the concept and reality of social change is nothing new for the elementary school and the elementary principal. What is new, however, is the rapidity and complexity of social change. The rapidity and complexity variables will continue to challenge the elementary principal.

The psychosocial model developed by Erik Erikson several decades ago remains relevant and applicable today. In his prolific work, Erikson identified eight age-specific crises every human being must encounter. These crises or conflicts, are unavoidable but resolved more effectively when caring people provide emotional stability and encouragement. Essentially, Erikson sees each crisis as a conflict between cognition and culture, a conflict never resolved to perfection. According to Erikson, a child's caretakers have great influence on the successful resolution of conflict through the first four phases of psychosocial development. The principal most certainly is one of those caretakers.[39]

The principal's own organization, The National Association of Elementary School Principals (N.A.E.S.P.), prepared a guide calling for more developmentally appropriate curriculum and instruction in the primary grades. This guide, titled, "Early Childhood Education and the Elementary School Principal: Standards for Quality Programs for Young Children," is available to N.A.E.S.P. members.[40]

Author Elliot Seif believes today's educational leaders should apply the organizational theories and concepts of Tom Peters to schools. The principals now responding to social change most likely would fit characteristics identified by Peters. These principals " . . . are responsive to the customer, create changes at a fast pace, are people centered. . ."[41] Seif concludes that school leaders must have characteristics that measure what is really important in school: listening, responsiveness, service, innovation, and support of failures.[42]

The elementary principal who is responding to social change most likely engages in what Joyce believes are the least common principal practices: focus on program and focus on student improvement.[43] The responsive-to-social-change principal must also be a caring person. As author Noddings suggests, the leader who is responding to social change is a leader who is not putting the ideal of caring at risk.[44]

The concept of caring is emerging as an important concept for educational leaders to consider. Recently the central theme of a series of articles in a leading educational journal was the theme of caring. A study on caring grew out of an experiment in a California school. The Child Development Project (CDP) begun in 1982, is devoted to teaching children to care. The results, to-date, suggest that by the time students reach sixth grade, they are not only displaying characteristics associated with caring but also outscoring control groups in higher order reading comprehension.[45] Indeed, author Kohn sees the absence of caring behavior among children " . . . reflected in the much-cited prevalence of teenage pregnancy and drug use but also in the evidence of rampant selfishness and competitiveness among young people."[46] The school is seen as the logical setting for the teaching of caring. This premise suggests children who learn to care will have had role models who care.[47]

The most recent study available regarding state policy and school principals appears to be one of the most promising studies to-date. Conducted by research teams in seven states, this study appears to be significant to the research of the author. This report, published by the Consortium of Policy Centers, was distributed by the Education Commission of the States. A summary includes a list of eleven state initiatives worth watching, several of which are relevant to this author's study.[48]

Studies of the principal as educational or instructional leader abound. These studies tend to focus on leadership style and staff development without including the principal's role in social change. Yet, staff development must now include the view that social change is a constant. The principal, through staff development, must establish a school culture that will adapt to and support on-going change.[49] Studies conducted since the 1920's suggest principals spend less time as educational leaders than they should. While principals say they want to be instructional leaders, they are finding the social-driven demands on the curriculum and the expansion of programs for at-risk students complicating their already complicated role. Researchers are suggesting the role of the contemporary principal be reexamined, perhaps even redefined. Otherwise, social and curricular demands will continue to create a climate for failure in our schools.

Characteristics

A major purpose of this study was to identify characteristics of principals who are responding to social change. One of the best-known assessments of a person's characteristic type is the *Myers-Briggs Type Inventory*. A data bank of more than 250,000 characteristic type scores includes the *MBTI* scores of educational leaders.[50] While several analyses of the *MBTI* scores of educational leaders are available, the author could not locate an analysis of scores of elementary principals separate from secondary principals. The following data, therefore, includes characteristic type identification of principals, both elementary and secondary combined.

According to the developers of the *MBTI*, there are four functions of conscious mental activity that pull people in different directions. These four functions are Sensation, Intuition, Thinking, and Feeling. Feeling types are people-oriented toward what matters to others. Feeling types make subjective decisions based on a combination of their own values as well as the values of others. There is a strong concern for human, not technical aspects to problems. Of the four functions associated with conscious mental activity in the direction of goals, the Feeling function is the only one that suggests caring. The Feeling function " . . . seeks rational order according to harmony among subjective values."[51]

An analysis of a study of the *MBTI* scores of 1,024 elementary and secondary principals revealed 50.30% are Feeling types. For comparative purposes, the author also analyzed the *MBTI* scores of 325 college and technical administrators. From this analysis, the author found 43.41% of the college and technical administrators are Feeling types.[52]

Data on occupations attractive to the sixteen characteristic types identified by *Myers-Briggs* researchers were analyzed by the author. The author will not discuss all sixteen characteristic types but rather cite the findings of two: Feeling/Judging types and Feeling/Perceptive types. According to [MBTI] data bank information, the highest percent of occupations atttractive to Feeling/Judging types was 17.79% for Clergy, all denominations.[53] Among the highest percent of occupations attractive to Feeling/Perceptive types were Rehabilitation Counselors (20.34%) and Psychologists (18.41%). Elementary and secondary principals were not among the highest percent of occupations associated with Feeling types.[54]

THE CHALLENGE OF SOCIAL CHANGE

Rapid social change will require school districts to employ principals who display characteristics like those associated with *MBTI*'s Feeling types as well as those associated with Nel Noddings' ideal of caring.

Concepts worth revisiting include the idea that educational systems tend to fall into, ". . . a role devoted exclusively to the conservation of old ideas, concepts, attitudes, skills and perceptions."[55] This educational role succeeds only when the environment is stable and fails when change is so rapid it becomes the primary characteristic of a society.[56] That social change in this nation is now the primary characteristic of that nation is an irrefutable concept, one that educational leaders must understand.

Even new ideas about educating young children growing up in the midst of tumultuous change often fail. The Beethoven Project is just one example of new ideas that fail because educational leaders are unprepared for their roles. In spite of millions and millions of taxpayer dollars intended to guarantee the success of The Beethoven Project, those in charge of the project concede failure. Poverty, fragmented families, and drug and alcohol problems are pervasive in the Chicago neighborhoods where the Beethoven Project was expected to perform miracles. Violence was commonplace. The media were critical of the seeming lack of progress for such a taxpayer-expensive project.[57] Elementary principals whose schools are fraught with social change problems must be careful not to promise miracles, much less short-term miracles. Expensive, innovative educational projects tend to attract the media which will scrutinize progress, especially when those projects are funded by the state or federal government.

A nationally known authority on children and learning is a prolific researcher and author on the subject of public education's role in early childhood. Dr. David Elkind is finding the schools appear to be changing in structure before our eyes. Elkind believes, however, the " . . . transformation of the school has come about not by a conscious pursuit of education reform but rather as an adaptive response to the changes in the family and in the larger society."[58] His theory is that the family is now what he calls "permeable," a postmodern form. This postmodern form is the result of decades of the school assuming more and more of the parents' role.[59]

Public education, in general, will continue to be called upon to offer solutions for all of society's ills and complexities. Bruce Joyce advises that a major restructuring of schools will require a " . . . transformation of the roles of all personnel and a reorientation of the norms of the workplace . . ."[60] Joyce also offers his thoughts on the effect this restructuring may have on others.

> So we begin the effort to create a system for the revamping of our education system, recognizing that the initiative will be regarded by some as a product of arrogance and by others as a sure sign of lunacy, but above all, that job will be hard.[61]

The "job" will be hard, indeed, because as research suggests, almost all school activities are structured as if all children live in lovely homes with intact families. While it is true that, no school can possibly compensate fully for inadequate parenting, poor nutrition, poor housing, and constant hopelessness fueled by drug-ridden, rat-infested neighborhoods, schools, nevertheless, will be expected to respond more effectively to the negative effects of social change.

A principal who is responding to social change as it impacts on children and their families as well as teachers and the teaching-learning process is most likely a caring person. Today's elementary schools must be led by a caring person who activates that caring by responding to the adverse effects of social change as they impact on school.

Today's elementary principal is and will continue to be a leader who is expected to address social change in positive ways. The concept of the principal as an agent of change emerged in the late 1970's, following numerous studies of the leader in the corporate world. This agent of change, or change agent, was originally described as a key person in business who, through innovation, responds to changes in the outside world by causing matching changes within the organization. Studies from the world of business were finding that within any organization, some people were able to cope with change better than others.[62] Three descriptors of key people within an organization who could be classified as change agents were, invariably, young, inexperienced and male.[63] The author was interested in whether today's change agent in the field of education meets the criteria of yesterday's change agent in the world of business: young, inexperienced and male. She thinks, it's not necessarily so!

The concept of change itself has been studied by theorists for decades. One of the best-known change theorists is Kurt Lewin. Lewin studied change and resistance to change in the 1940's and his findings have withstood the tests of time and challenge. Educational leaders, among them elementary principals, have been students of Lewin's "force-field analysis"[64] and "targeting process."[65] While these constructs are important for elementary principals to understand during their response to social change, these constructs are only peripherally relevant to this study. More relevant to this study are the perceptions of Mark Hanson, who connects the human costs of change with staff development:

> The costs of change that involve traditions or sacred cows of a school will be unacceptable to many and thus provocative of resistance.[66]

The elementary principal who is responding in positive ways to social change as it impacts on staff as well as children and parents will be demonstrating success in meeting and overcoming resistance to change.

Today's elementary principals, male or female, younger or older, experienced or inexperienced, are surely feeling the myriad effects of social change in their schools. One such effect, directly related to social change, is a significant increase in special needs students. The learning disability (LD) population, alone, has increased 140% over the last ten years.[67] Research indicates, "Children who have been maimed by such new social epidemics as homelessness and crack use by pregnant women are already testing the resources and tolerance of the schools."[68]

The social issues of poverty, single parents, mothers in the workforce, child care, child abuse, cultural diversity, and drug and alcohol abuse will continue to impact on the child as a learner in school. Perhaps the most negative effect on the learner as a school student will come from the social issue of poverty. There is new evidence that poverty and learning problems in school go hand-in-hand. University of Georgia researchers discovered a high correlation between teacher identification of academically at-risk students and the criterion of free and/or reduced price lunch. Researchers Payne and Payne asked elementary teachers in one school to identify students they considered academically at-risk. The teachers identified 495 students or 66% of the school population. The reason most frequently given by teachers as to why students were academically at-risk was "Unsupportive home environment," which included economics as well as parenting skills.[69] While three criteria were examined — grade retention, reading and reading-related achievement tests, and free and/or reduced price lunch — the criterion most strongly correlated with students academically at-risk was free and/or reduced price lunch. Phi coefficients were .79 (p < .05), findings the researchers considered uniformly high.[70]

As a result of a review of the literature and this author/educator's own experiences with the impact of social change on public education, this study appears to be timely. The elementary principal will be required to lead children, teachers and parents into the 21st century. Due to rapid social change, the elementary principal will need to be a more responsive leader. More responsive elementary principals will almost surely mean better quality elementary programs, procedures and staff development. Children are the beneficiaries; their inheritance, therefore, will depend a great deal on the responsiveness of educational leaders. At the elementary level, that person is the principal.

IV

The Design of the Study

The author chose descriptive research to carry out the study. Descriptive research is concerned with "what is."[71] An example of descriptive research in education is Sara Lightfoot's study of high schools recognized for their excellence. From Lightfoot's study of "what is" emerged a book, *The Good High School*.[72] Unquestionably, descriptive research is an exhaustive search for a kernel of truth. According to Paul Leedy, descriptive research is:

> ". . . a very 'busy' research method from the standpoint of the researcher. Therein lies the element of danger. It demands more activity than perhaps other methodologies.It is also probably the most complex of all the research methodologies."[73]

Descriptive research is, today, a more acceptable methodology than it was in the past. Years ago, one of the leaders of educational research found it, ". . . lacking in precision and often hopelessly vague . . . "[74] Even today, researchers in the biological and physical sciences see experimental research as superior to the descriptive method. Researcher Leedy came to the defense of descriptive research when he wrote that research has to be an all-out offensive against our ignorance of the truth, wherever that ignorance may live.[75]

DATA COLLECTION

Descriptions and Procedures

This author believes the best offensive against an ignorance of the truth lies in the methodology of descriptive research. This method was best-suited to the purpose of the study which was to identify activities and characteristics of principals who are responding to social change as it impacts on the elementary school. What matters most to the author is that educators and educational leaders not become so discouraged by the statistics of social change that they simply give up or give in. There can be no giving up or giving in! Where, oh where in this country are elementary principals who have not allowed social change statistics to render them helpless? Most certainly, elementary principals like Martin and Meredith can teach us what to do by their example. We need to study other elementary principals who are now engaged in activities and programs that are positively affecting their schools. Descriptive research seems to be the perfect avenue to travel for getting us moving in the right direction.

The study included an invitation telephone call to identified principals, an in-person interview, and a characteristic identification tool. In advance of the interview, the principal was asked by the author to complete the characteristic identification tool, the *Myers-Briggs Type Indicator (MBTI)*, *Form G*. Prior to selecting the *Myers-Briggs*, the author analyzed both Form*s F* and *G* and found *Form G* more suitable because it is a shorter version. *Form G* can be completed in fifteen to twenty minutes with the same results as the longer version. [76]

The *MBTI* is based on the perception and judgment theories of C.G Jung. The four basic indices are: Extroverted/Introverted, Sensing/Intuition, Thinking/Feeling, and Judging/Perceiving. From those four basic indices emerge 16 types or characteristics.[77] The author described the MBTI to each principal when she telephoned to invite the principal to participate in the study. She received the principal's agreement to complete the *MBTI* in advance of the interview. The principal also agreed to a one-to-one-and-a-half-hour interview during which time the author would ask questions about the principal and social change. It was understood that the elementary principals could not possibly be addressing equally all seven social change issues the author had identified. Research design, therefore, reflected this understanding.

Research questions were answered through the interview questions. The interview questions are part of the instrument. Twice during the interview, the researcher discussed confidentiality with the principal. Further, the researcher explained the principal would be referred to as Principal *A* or another letter name and that the name of the principal's school, school district, or county would not be revealed.

Construction of the Instrument

Through all research design components, the author hoped to gain a broader perspective of the problem. An interview approach allowed the author to enter the principal's world, in person, in order to acquire information that could not be acquired in other ways. Bruno Bettelheim's words are appropriate to quote at this time as they support the author's belief that one learns best about a person when meeting with that person where he or she lives. Bettelheim said, "When I enter a school, I can sense its ambience, much like entering a home."[78]

An interview approach was well-suited to this study because it allowed the author to engage in a series of ". . . friendly conversations in which the investigator gradually introduces new elements in order to gain the information sought."[79] The study was designed to gain an immediate and comfortable rapport with the interviewee before pursuing the more personal and subjective part of the interview.

According to educational research authors, the interview method is selected in order to uncover information that cannot be directly observed. Qualitative research, through the interview method, has one main purpose and that is to discover what is on and in somebody else's mind.[80] In order to uncover information that could not be directly observed and to discover what was on and in principals' minds, the author's interview questions were designed to include all six types of interview questions recommended by authorities: Opinion/Value, Demographic/Background, Experience/Behavior, Sensory, Feelings, and Knowledge.[81]

The Pilot Study

A pilot study was conducted in order to assist the author in making refinements to the design and instrument before the actual study began. The pilot study was conducted in a county in south-eastern Pennsylvania two weeks prior to the beginning of the actual study. Three elementary principals employed in that county were identified by the same panel of educational leaders who identified social responsive principals in the three counties selected for the actual study. The rationale for selecting the pilot study county was two-fold: the pilot study county is contiguous with two of the three counties identified for the actual study; socio-economic factors in the pilot study county and the three counties identified for the study are similar.

All data were gathered in a one month period in order to strengthen internal consistency.

POPULATION

There are 1,635 public school elementary principals in the state of Pennsylvania. Of that number, 1,599 or 98%, have at least a Master's degree.

The population of this study was ten elementary principals recognized as responding in positive ways to the negative effects of social change. All ten principals were employed in public schools in three southeastern Pennsylvania counties. According to the most recent data from Pennsylvania's Department of Education, a total of ninety-six public school elementary principals are employed in those three counties.

A panel of educational leaders identified twelve principals as principals who were responding to social change as it impacted on their schools. Of those twelve, eight were males and four were females. Those twelve principals represented 12% of the potential population of sixty-eight males and twenty-eight females.

The author invited all twelve identified elementary principals to participate in the study. During a preliminary telephone call, it was discovered one female functioning as a principal was not certified as an elementary principal but rather a certified elementary supervisor. As a result of lack of principal certification, the author eliminated this "functioning" principal from the population to be studied. One male elementary principal met the criteria for participation in the study but declined because he was in the process of closing three elementary buildings and opening a brand new school.

The gender make-up of elementary principals in the three Pennsylvania counties in which the study took place is sixty-eight males and twenty-eight females for a ratio of 7:3. The gender make-up of elementary principals in the state of Pennsylvania is 1,133 males and 495 females for a male-female ratio of 7:3.[82]

The gender make-up of elementary principals who participated in the study was identical to the state gender make-up: seven males and three females for a ratio of 7:3. The author made no attempt to produce a proportionate representation of males and females such as exists within the three counties in which the study took place. A proportionate representation, nevertheless, did occur.

Procedures for Establishing Population

The population was established from names of elementary principals recognized by educational leaders as responding to social change as it impacted on their respective schools. All responsive-to-social change public school elementary principals in three counties had an equal chance of being recognized by a panel of educational leaders. A panel of educational leaders was made up of administrators whose chief responsibility was programming and staff development. The educational leaders who formed the panel were employed by an Intermediate Unit and not by a school district. The author discussed the purpose of her study with the panel before asking them to recommend principals for the study. The author defined for the panel the term "social change" and listed the seven social change issues she had identified. Further, she described how elementary principals might be responding through programs, procedures, and staff development.

Within one week of initial contact with each panel member, the panel provided the author with the names and telephone numbers of principals who appeared to be ideal candidates for the study. The panel members never received from the author a suggested minimum or maximum number of principal-names to submit. The author instead intended to select, at random, the names of ten, eleven, or twelve principals from the total submitted by the panel of educational leaders. Since the names of the principals submitted totalled twelve, the author decided to include all twelve in the study. A random selection, therefore, was unnecessary. Ultimately, the population was reduced to 10 because one principal was not state certified and another was more over-worked than the others at that moment in time and was unable to participate.

The Intermediate Units of Pennsylvania

There are 29 different Intermediate Units in Pennsylvania, established to provide educational services to all school districts in the state. Some Intermediate Units provide services for several counties while others provide services for just one county. One of the counties in the study shares an Intermediate Unit with another county not part of the study. The other two counties in the study receive exclusive services from their own Intermediate Unit. A map of the Intermediate Units in Pennsylvania is included in the Appendix.

The establishment of population validity is necessary in qualitative research whenever the researcher intends to generalize her findings. With a relatively small population, however, this author is unable to generalize her findings. Nevertheless, she attempted to establish population validity.

THE INSTRUMENT

Development of the Instrument

The instrument was designed to gather both qualitative and quantitative data. The heart of the study, however, was qualitative research. In developing the instrument, the author considered elements of the case study so that data gathered could be, in part, arranged in case study format. Educational researchers now consider the case study and qualitative research almost synonymous.[83]

While in the past, quantitative educational research was almost always required, the trend today, ". . . is to collect both qualitative and quantitative data.[84] Educational researchers of today no longer believe qualitative observations are necessary only when new knowledge is being developed.[85]

Description of the Instrument

The instrument was designed to enable the author to focus on a single problem through combinations of data. The interview format was used as well as the *Myers-Briggs Type Indicator, Form G*. The author chose the interview format since authorities in the field noted that an interview of one individual can gain more understanding about a researcher's topic than ". . . a shallow survey of 100 subjects."[86] The author chose *MBTI, Form G* for four reasons: its purpose correlated well with the purpose of this study, reliability and validity were well-documented over more than two decades, the questions were considered non-threatening, and the principal could complete it within 20 minutes.

MBTI internal consistency was derived from product-moment correlations of X and Y continuous scores with Spearman-Brown prophecy formula correction. Samples of subjects from a wide range of ages, occupations and personality types were measured for test-retest agreement. Test-retest product-moment correlations were described in samples where subjects ranged from seventh grade through medical school. Seven tables examine *MBTI* reliability.[87] Reliability studies indicate that samples of older people have higher reliability estimates than samples of younger people.[88]

Regarding validity, the *MBTI* correlates well with other well-known measures as *Personality Research Inventory*, *Kuder Occupational Interest Survey* and *Kolb Learning Style Inventory*.[89] Validity data indicate *MBTI* scores are consistent with behavior predicted by theory, specifically the theory of C.J. Jung.[90]

The interview component of the author's instrument required approximately one to one-and-a-half hours to complete. Questions in Part I of the interview were constructed to put the principal at ease by exploring what the principal's school was doing about social change. Part II of the interview was constructed to gather demographic types of data, including professional and personal information. The most personal data about the principal were gathered in Part II. This technique was recommended by authorities on the interview method of data gathering.[91] The *MBTI* assessment was the third and final part of the instrument although the *MBTI* was actually completed by the principals in advance of the interview.

All stages of the development of the instrument were influenced by the findings of authorities on educational research. During the first stage of instrument development, the author internalized Leedy's words, "Like oil beneath the sea, the first problem is to devise a tool to probe below the surface."[92] During subsequent stages of the development of the instrument, the author considered Fetterman's "whole trait complex," a means to discover broad patterns instead of a few characteristics.[93] The researcher also considered Goetz' recommendation that demographic type questions be intermingled with others rather than clustered in one area only. Goetz' rationale is that demographic questions are less interesting than other kinds of questions.[94]

Parts I and II of the instrument are included in the Appendix. The *Myers-Briggs Type Inventory, Form G*, may not be reproduced for inclusion in the Appendix.

Data Collection

Descriptive research is the method which requires the technique of observation as the primary means of data collection. The author was extremely careful not to introduce bias into the design of the study. Data were safeguarded from the influence of research bias during data collection.[95]

Data were gathered by the author during the interview and through the scores on the *MBTI*. The data gathered during the pre-screening telephone call were saved for reference during the analysis phase of the project.

Maintaining internal validity was essential during the collection and analysis of data. Four kinds of extraneous variables pose a threat to internal validity: history, experimental mortality, maturation and instrumentation.[96] The author believed only one variable was a potential threat to her study: instrumentation. Every precaution, therefore, was taken to avoid recording errors while using the instrument.

All data were gathered during the interview, including the completed-in-advance *MBTI*, in order to strengthen internal validity. The most common way to record interview data is by tape-recording so that all information can be saved for later analysis. A combination approach, however, was initially perceived by the author to be the better recording method. A combination approach would have found the author writing down what was being said while also tape-recording.[97] This approach was believed to offer the author a solid data base; however, the pilot study participants recommended the author refrain from using a tape recorder. They were unanimous in recommending the author use shorthand as the only recording method.

The data gathering process required no written response from the principal except in the completion of the *MBTI*. The author placed a code at the top right corner of each interview sheet. This code served two purposes: to maintain principal anonymity and to assist the author in matching data sheets should they become separated during processing.

The principal's verbal responses were hand-recorded by the author. Since the author writes 120 words per minute in shorthand, she recorded, with ease, everything the principals said and transcribed her notes later with almost 100% accuracy. Only once did she need to telephone a principal for clarification of a term used by that principal during the interview. Using shorthand was a successful way for the author to maintain eye contact with an interviewee while she wrote. By the author's use of shorthand, the interviewee was able to maintain his or her normal conversational speed throughout the entire interview. In following the above procedures, the author avoided the disadvantages of note-taking, which concern some research authorities.[98]

Before the interview began, the author assured the principal she would maintain confidentiality. She also offered to provide the Principal with the results of the completed study.

A pilot study is recommended whenever a researcher chooses an interview or questionnaire format.[99] This author's instrument, therefore, was used in a pilot study so that refinements could be made prior to the actual study.

The instrument is part of the Appendix.

Data Analysis

According to authorities, "Data do not constitute Absolute Truth, but merely a behavioral manifestation of the Truth."[100] Through an analysis of the data gleaned from the interview, however, the author hoped to find more truth revealed than if she had pursued truth through a mailed questionnaire.

Data collected by the author were processed in the following way:

First, quantifiable data were recorded and analyzed. Second, all data from instrument Parts I, II and III were written in narrative form, much like a case study. Each principal was treated as an individual recognized by educational leaders as responding to social change as it impacted on the elementary school. In this way, there was an attempt to understand each principal holistically, apart from the others in the study. Within twenty-four hours of each principal interview, data were recorded and stored in the author's Macintosh computer. Data analysis, therefore, was begun within a day of the author's final principal interview.

After all data were written in narrative form and all quantifiable data were recorded, the author identified common activities and characteristics among all principals in the sample. Throughout all phases of data processing, the author searched for patterns of activities and characteristics of the responsive-to-social change principals whose leadership had not placed the "ideal of caring at risk."[101]

During all stages of data treatment, the author kept in mind that she is, ". . . in a factual dungeon. He (she) will never be able to see the source of the data. We glibly talk of populations made up of individuals. But the *individual* — the person 'inside' — we shall never know!"[102] Researchers, however, will never completely believe they will never know.

Once all data were recorded and analyzed, the author compiled all findings in a report. Descriptive statistics were used. Tables were included for visual enhancement of the data.

V

Results of the Study

The purpose of this study was to identify activities and characteristics of principals who are responding in positive ways to the negative effects of social change as they impact on the elementary school. Before the author could identify principal-characteristics, however, she first had to discover what principals were doing in response to social change.

Ten elementary principals participated in the study. The author gathered data through an in-person interview and the *Myers-Briggs Type Inventory, Form G*. All data were gathered over a one month period. Once all data were recorded, the author began to analyze the data in order to answer the seven research questions which follow.

RESEARCH QUESTIONS

Question 1

What is the elementary principal doing, through programs, procedures and staff development, to respond to the negative effects of social change as they impact on the elementary school?

This question contained seven social issues components: Poverty, Single Parent Families, Mothers in the Workforce, Child Care, Child Abuse, Cultural Diversity, and Drug and Alcohol Abuse. Each component was analyzed separately.

A. *Poverty*

Each of the ten principals interviewed expressed concern about an increase in "poor" children among their students. The percent of students living at the poverty level was determined by the percent of students receiving free or reduced price lunch. The author found a range of 8% to 95% of students living in poverty. While poverty was a very serious problem for two urban principals (85% and 95% of the school population), a poverty trend was perceived among all principals, even the principal whose poverty students were only 8% of the school population. Seven principals reported they were actively involved in collecting clothing, food baskets, and funds for school supplies and field trips for children and families in need. Six principals reported an aggressive effort in "going after" whatever was needed to give each student in the school an equal opportunity to gain access to a good education and an elevated self-esteem.

Table 1 will indicate the percent of the principals' students living in poverty. The author found the best way to measure poverty in each principal's school was to use the school's statistics on "free or reduced price lunch."

TABLE 1

School Population and Student Poverty

Principal	No. of Students	% of students in poverty
A	710	15%
B	650	8%
C	424	19%
D	476	15%
E	460	25%
F	651	95%
G	536	14%
H	519	25%
I	720	85%
J	570	40%

Each of the ten principals mentioned the school nurse as a key person addressing health and nutrition as it relates to the children living in poor families. Six principals used superlatives in describing the work of their school nurses. All but one principal had a guidance counselor to assist with behavioral problems associated with poverty. All principals expressed the belief that the needs of parents living in poverty or near poverty must be addressed if their children are going to remain in school and receive a good education.

Every principal was able to offer several examples of projects undertaken by home-school associations as well as unpublicized, discreet efforts of teachers and other school employees on behalf of poor students. To a principal, a theme of anonymity in order to offer children and parents help with dignity was evident. As one principal expressed, "These children and their parents have their pride."

Below are four examples of principals' comments on their involvement in the area of poverty:

Principal B: "Our PTO raised $22,000 profit from a cookie sale. No child ever misses a field trip or anything. Money is there for any child who needs something badly, whether clothing or school supplies. It's a quiet thing."

Principal D: "We are beginning to get poor children in this school. More of our parents are in and out of the workforce. Some homes have no hot water. We have two showers in the school for kids who need them. Our nurse gets them in and out of the shower and into the classroom without anyone knowing about it. I'm not sure many people know about this and that's what we want."

Principal G: "Our home-school association buys sweat suits and we give them out to kids who don't have appropriate clothes to wear. Churches donate hats, mittens and gloves. Teachers and I get together for kids who don't have coats and ask mothers whose children have outgrown theirs to donate them. All we have to say to our home-school association is, 'We have kids who don't have money for this or that.' They always come through, no matter what is needed."

Principal I: "With 85% on free or reduced lunch, health and nutrition is a real issue. Our nurse knows the kids who come to school unfed. The teachers or I will check them out and send them to the nurse for something to eat. Our parent group buys cereal. The nurse feeds cereal to the kids. Nobody knows although those kids we feed do come in late for class, that's all. We have a real good parent group, even though the parents are all poor. Throughout the year, we collect tons of clothing and give away bags of groceries. We do all this as part of our commitment to kids."

All principals interviewed expressed special concern for the youngest children, that is, primary grade children, in their school community. Head Start programs, as well as the relatively new Even Start Program, were established in the urban schools. Two urban and three suburban-school principals reported they offer preschool Story Time and a newsletter for parents of preschoolers.

All principals reported their school provides a kindergarten screening before children are formally enrolled in kindergarten. All principals reported children who demonstrated a developmental lag, often poverty-related, were recommended for some kind of appropriate intervention. Five principals reported their schools offer intervention strategies in the form of a developmental kindergarten or a transitional first or second grade. Poverty as it impacts on early childhood education was a priority issue with all principals who participated in the study.

B. *Single Parent Families*

All principals reported their school curriculum is beginning to address single parent families and other non-traditional families. Seven principals discussed specific areas of the curriculum where the non-traditional family is explored, for example social studies, literature and a guidance program. Three principals feel their teachers must more consciously build non-traditional family concepts into the curriculum. One rural principal said it is his job to ". . . make sure the staff knows of the growing numbers of single parent families. For example, last year, fifty to sixty-two percent of our kindergartners came from single-parent homes and the teachers had to understand what that means to the curriculum." Another principal said, "I coach teachers to say, 'Your family' instead of 'Your mother or father.' Many, many children in this school have different last names than their parents." A third principal said, "Our social studies and guidance programs teach the concept that your family consists of people you live with. Your family might be your mom and your aunt or your dad and his friend."

All principals reported evening parent conferences were provided for single parents who could not attend daytime parent conferences. All principals used the word "flexibility" in describing the scheduling of parent conferences for single-parent families. One principal said single parents get "first shot" at evening conferences. Three principals said they make sure non-custodial parents are given the opportunity to meet with their child's teacher. One principal said teachers first schedule conferences with the non-custodial parent so that the parent can look through the child's papers before they are taken home by the custodial parent.

Five principals reported free sitter service was offered during evening parent conferences. The remaining five said their staff provides puzzles, games, and other activities for the children who must accompany their parents to conferences. All principals said they totally accept the fact that many children must accompany their parent or parents to teacher-parent conferences.

One principal exemplified the feelings of the other principals interviewed in regard to the single-parent family. "We run into unusual family structures and we try to be respectful. When a boyfriend comes to school with a child's mother, I say, 'I recognize so-and-so's mother but I'd like to know who you are.' The boy friend introduces himself and everyone is put at ease. I just treat him as a part of what's going on."

Single parent families are becoming more common to principals each new school year. The principals participating in the study estimated between 20% to 75% of their students live in single parent families. While mothers tend to be the head of single parent families, the principals reported an increase in the number of fathers who are gaining custody of their children. Teacher acceptance of the single parent family as just one of several contemporary family structures was perceived by the principal as essential. Helping the more traditional teachers to accept the single parent family as a fact of life was seen by the principals as a major staff development project.

C. *Mothers in the Workforce*

All principals interviewed saw child care as the main problem for mothers in the workforce. All principals made sure bus transportation was provided to a day care center or a sitter's house, so long as the bus stop was within district boundaries.

Only one principal reported the school district operated its own after-school latch key program, through the district's recreation program. Three principals reported their students can receive child care through the YMCA.; school bus transportation was provided. Two principals reported the YMCA will be operating a child care program for their schools next fall. One principal described the child care program he/she helped establish sixteen years ago in a local church. Presently this program serves three, four and five-year olds but will expand to after-school care in the Fall.

Only one principal reported his/her school has no child care plans for the future. This principal, however, described the ways the school attempts to help parents locate baby-sitters in the community.

The social issue of mothers in the workforce is impacting on the elementary school in numerous ways. The principals identified one of their greatest concerns as young students who must care for themselves both before and after school because their mothers are at work. As a result, young children often arrive at school in the morning unkempt, hungry, and inappropriately dressed for weather conditions. The school nurse, counselors, and classroom teachers are encouraged by the principal to provide these children with both physical and emotional nurturing.

D. *Child Care*

The author discovered the social issue of child care is inextricably tied to the social issue of mothers in the workforce. Principals' responses to mothers-in-the-workforce questions, therefore, answered most of the author's child care questions. Nonetheless, the author wanted to establish that the social issues of Mothers in the Workforce and Child Care are not synonymous since custodial fathers also need child care services. The majority of principals made references to the difficulty some of the fathers were having in locating child care when the "sitter," frequently the paternal grandmother or aunt, decided to seek employment outside the home.

All principals supported child care programs for their students within the school setting or within the community. One principal said, "Transportation to day care centers and baby-sitters is just routine." Another principal said, "If the sitter's house happens to be outside the district and we have a bus going nearby, we twist arms and we adjust. We do everything we can." A third principal remarked, "I personally believe we should be providing child care in our school. I'm hoping this will happen. It will be better for kids. We know how to take care of them."

Clearly, the principal who is responding to social change is accepting of child care as a norm for the present and future. None of the ten principals participating in the study suggested nor demonstrated a philosophical conflict with the concept of child care as a need to be met beyond the family. All ten principals said they welcome or would welcome a child care program in their school. Only one principal expressed concern that, in time, public schools might find themselves more in the child care business than in the education business.

E. *Child Abuse*

Child abuse is a social issue which visibly disturbed each principal interviewed. All ten principals reported an increase in suspected child-abuse cases. All ten principals said neglect is a form of child abuse.

In Pennsylvania, the law is clear about school personnel reporting suspected child abuse to a "Hot Line" agency, usually Children and Youth Services. Children and Youth Services is an agency created and funded by the state. A report, usually through a telephone call, must be made to Children and Youth Services personnel by the principal or the principal's designee. The principal's designee is, most often, the school nurse or counselor. School employees are breaking the law whenever they do not report suspected child abuse. The name of the school employee reporting suspected child abuse is never to be disclosed to a parent.

Each principal described the procedures followed whenever child abuse is suspected. The author's questions differentiated between procedures followed for neglect and procedures followed for physical abuse (including sexual abuse). The majority of principals (eight) said they followed different procedures for physical abuse and neglect. These principals tended to address neglect behind the scenes, over time, and with assistance from the community. Physical abuse, however, was addressed immediately by calling the "Hot Line." All ten principals said the Hot Line telephone number they called was to Children and Youth Services. Eight of the ten principals interviewed said they called Children and Youth Services as soon as the nurse and/or the guidance counselor convinced the principal that the abuse occurred. Two of the principals interviewed said they called the parents first if child abuse was never before suspected. Their rationale was that parents ought to be given the benefit of the doubt, at least the first time they were suspected of abusing their child.

Principals unanimously stated they were satisfied with the way their school was handling suspected child abuse. Principals also stated, unanimously, that they were dissatisfied with the way Children and Youth Services handled situations once they left the responsibility of the school. Two common criticisms of Children and Youth Services among all principals interviewed were: [1] schools are uninformed about the child in that abusive situation and not privy to a course of action; as a result, teachers, nurses, counselors and principals are not sure how to respond to the child. [2] neglect is ignored by Children and Youth Services; they don't even want to hear about neglect.

One principal summed up the other principals' frustrations when he said, "Schools aren't doing a very good job in the area of neglect. There are a lot of kids I consider to be neglected but when we go to Children and Youth Services, they tell us right away they don't have time to deal with this. They say it might be neglect to us but to the parents it's just values. I disagree!"

Two urban principals said they now called the police department at City Hall whenever children were still at school at 5:30 P.M. because their parents failed to pick them up. These principals said calling City Hall was one way to get parents cited for neglect.

Eight of ten principals interviewed described serious cases of child abuse in their schools. Three principals discussed child- abuse prevention assembly programs their schools offered. Parents were informed in advance of these programs and invited to attend. Following these programs, "safe areas in the school" were identified and students were encouraged to go to those "safe areas" if they wanted to talk with someone about abuse. A program mentioned by two principals was Giggles the Clown. Both principals made positive comments about this program. One principal mentioned an effective program offered by the Rape Crisis Center.

Clearly, child abuse was the most difficult social issue for the principals to discuss. Principals spoke of child abuse in emotional voices. The fact that child abuse not only existed in the homes of their students but also increased in numbers of cases was a dual fact the principals said they abhorred.

F. *Cultural Diversity*

Three urban principals, two suburban principals, and one rural principal described their efforts in the area of cultural diversity to a much greater degree than did the other four principals. While all principals interviewed stated cultural diversity was a social issue that needed to be addressed in all schools, not all principals felt cultural diversity was an issue they could focus upon at present. One principal said his/her school was so homogeneous, the absence of cultural diversity was a problem. When asked to elaborate on that statement, the principal cited examples of prejudice and intolerance among students for anyone "different."

Six of the principals described the ways they are committed to their school's acceptance of differences among cultures. All six of those principals said their teachers must demonstrate and teach acceptance through understanding. Two urban principals said teachers who do not demonstrate acceptance of different cultures are not asked to return to their schools the following year. This is not to say teachers who do not accept cultural differences among students are fired, but rather transferred to another school the following year.

Cultural diversity was a major social issue to five principals and a minor social issue to four. The absence of cultural diversity was somewhat of a cultural diversity intolerance problem for one principal.

G. *Drugs and Alcohol*

All principals stated the consequences of drug and alcohol abuse were felt within their schools. Eight principals said they believe growing numbers of their youngest students have been damaged in the womb by drugs, alcohol or both. These principals cited childrens' medical history records as verifying their suspicions that increased numbers of chemical-damaged children are coming to school. These principals spoke of growing numbers of their youngest students (pre-kindergarten through second grade) who needed special education programs or special assistance within the regular classroom.

Drug and alcohol prevention programs began in the schools of all ten principals by second grade. Six principals reported the grade for beginning drug and alcohol prevention programs was kindergarten. The program used by seven principals, "Here's Looking at you, 2000," was developed by an organization called Chemical Health Education Foundation. Assemblies on the dangers of drugs and alcohol were held for students in six principals' schools. Special seminars and presentations were offered for the parents in six principals' schools. Programs coordinated with local police were described by two principals.

Nine of ten principals were actively involved with numerous programs and projects aimed at educating their students about drugs and alcohol and focusing on prevention. Eight of ten principals said they felt their drug and alcohol prevention programs were just now making a positive impact. The consensus of the principals was that their schools were doing a decent job in the area of drug and alcohol education.

SUMMARY

The author identified seven social issues which now impact on the elementary school: Poverty, Single Parent Family, Mothers in the Workforce, Child Care, Child Abuse, Cultural Diversity, and Drug and Alcohol Abuse. After each principal discussed each social issue, the author wanted to know to which social issue the principal was responding most and least.

A single social issue to which the majority of principals were responding most was not clearly identified. Four principals (40%) felt they were most responsive to single parent families. Six principals (60%) expressed difficulty in naming a single social change issue to which they were responding most. One explanation for this difficulty, expressed by the principals themselves, was the belief that priority social issues were in a constant state of change, according to the ever-changing needs of children and families. After a relatively long period of reflection, four principals stated they could not choose a single social issue as the one to which they were responding most. As a result, all four chose two social issues. The social issue to which the principals responded *least* was readily named. Six principals (60%) felt they were least responsive to cultural diversity within their schools.

Nine principals could identify a single social issue to which they were responding least while only six could identify a single social issue to which they were responding most. Just one principal decided to name two social issues as those he/she was responding to least.

Table 2 examines the social issues to which the principal is responding both most and least. While the author neither invited nor encouraged the principals to identify more than one social issue for each category, four principals, nevertheless, identified two.

TABLE 2

Social Issues To Which Principals are Responding Most and Least

Principal	Responding Most	Responding Least
A	Single Parents	Cultural Diversity
B	Child Abuse/Drug Abuse	Child Care
C	Single Parents	Child Care
D	Mothers in Workforce	Cultural Diversity
E	Mothers in Workforce	Cultural Diversity
F	Cultural Diversity	Poverty
G	Single Parents	Cultural Diversity
H	Single Parents/Drug Abuse	Cultural Diversity
I	Poverty/Cultural Diversity	Mothers in Workforce/ Cultural Diversity
J	Poverty/Cultural Diversity	Drug Abuse

As would be expected, the three urban principals participating in the study selected cultural diversity as the social issue to which they were responding most. One urban principal said he was most and least responsive to cultural diversity. His explanation for this seeming contradiction was that while he was responding most to cultural diversity, he perceived that response as not good enough; therefore, he also judged himself as being least responsive to the social issue of cultural diversity. The author felt a responsibility to report this principal's response, even though it may be confusing to the reader.

None of the suburban and rural school principals said they were responding most to cultural diversity. Five of six suburban and rural school principals selected cultural diversity as the social issue to which they were responding least.

Question 2

Are there similarities between the principal's present school and his or her childhood school?

Like people, schools have characteristics. A school has characteristics which include type of school and socio-economic make-up of the student population. Three types of schools were identified by the author: rural, suburban, and urban. The socio-economic make-up of a school population included three categories: lower class, middle class, and upper class.

For seven principals, the type of school they attended as children was different from the type of school their present students attend. Only three principals reported attending the same type school as their present students. Of the ten principals interviewed, one urban principal attended an urban school as a child; one suburban principal attended a suburban school as a child; one rural principal attended a rural school as a child.

A majority of the principals, six, reported growing up in a family with lower class status. The remaining four principals reported growing up in a middle class family. No principal reported growing up in an upper class family. The majority of principals who participated in the study said they could identify with their present students in terms of poverty or near-poverty.

Three comparative choices were offered the principals in regard to their childhood classmates' socio-economic status and their present students' socio-economic status. A majority of the principals (seven) reported the socio-economic status of their childhood classmates was similar or very similar to the socio-economic status of their present students.

Table 3 describes types of schools and socio-economic status of both principals and their students.

TABLE 3

Principal's Present School Compared with Principal's Childhood School

Principal	Present School	Childhood School Status	Childhood Socio-economic Comparison	Socio-economic
A	Rural	Urban	Lower class	Very similar
B	Suburban	Suburban	Middle class	Similar
C	Suburban	Urban	Middle class	Similar
D	Rural	Suburban	Middle class	Different
E	Suburban	Urban	Lower class	Similar
F	Urban	Urban	Lower class	Similar
G	Rural	Rural	Middle class	Similar
H	Rural	Urban	Lower class	Very different
I	Urban	Rural	Lower class	Very similar
J	Urban	Suburban	Lower class	Different

While the type of school the principals attended as children was usually different from the the type of school where they are presently the principal, the socio-economic status of their childhood classmates and their present students was similar. All principals demonstrated an ability to identify with the difficulties students caught in the middle of social change issues were experiencing.

Question 3

Are there similarities in the family structure of the principal and his or her students? Family structure includes socio-economic status, mother-father relationship, number of siblings and birth order positioning.

The author explored the principal's childhood family structure as well as the principal's present family structure before focusing on the principal's students and their families. While the principals perceived similarities in the socio-economic status of their childhood classmates and their present students, their childhood family structure was considerably different from the family structure of their students. All ten principals grew up in homes headed by their biological mother and father, whereas, all principals reported an already large and still-growing number of their students living with one parent. According to the ten principals studied, approximately 20% to 75% of their students lived in single-parent homes.

All principals listed the members of their childhood families in order of birth, beginning with the oldest family member. In all cases, the principal lived, as a child, with both mother and father. Regarding the principal's ordinal position within the family, four were first born, three were in the middle of relatively large families, two were youngest and one was an only child. There was no second-born nor classic middle child (middle of three) among the principals. Two principals grew up in families where there were seven children. One of those two principals was youngest of seven children and the other was fifth of seven. The ten childhood families of the principals studied produced a total of forty-one children.

The principals' present family structure was different from their present students' family structure in several ways. All principals reported they were married and living with their original spouse. All male principals (seven) were married and have children. All female principals (three) were married with no children. The present families of the principals studied produced a total of fourteen children, as contrasted with their childhood families, which produced forty-one children.

The principal's present and childhood family structures were different from the family structure of the majority or growing majority of their students. Despite the differences between the principal's family structures, past and present, and his or her students' family structure, the principal demonstrates an acceptance of these differences.

Question 4

Who will the principal remember as people who are/were caring individuals?

The principals were asked two questions regarding caring people.

When asked in which grade they first came upon the teacher who really cared about students, most principals (seven) identified teachers from fourth through seventh grade. A fifth grade teacher was identified by three principals as the first caring teacher they came across. A first grade teacher was identified by two female principals. A second grade teacher was identified by one female principal. All female principals, therefore, reported primary teachers as their first caring teacher while all male principals reported intermediate level or junior high teachers as their first caring teacher.

Three male principals expressed anger over their own elementary school experience. They found elementary school an uncomfortable, even hostile place where they felt uncared for and unaccepted by teachers. Their comments and the retelling of their own experiences as elementary students were emotion-laden.

The second "caring" question asked the principals was in regard to the most caring person they ever knew. In all instances (ten) the principals identified someone other than their first caring teacher. This question was far more difficult for all principals to answer than it was for all to identify their first caring teacher.

Table 4 examines both the first caring teacher encountered by the principal and the most caring person the principal has ever known.

TABLE 4

Principal's Naming of Caring People

Principal	First Caring Teacher	Most Caring Person Ever Known
A	5th grade	A colleague
B	6th grade	Wife
C	2nd grade	Mother
D	5th grade	Father
E	5th grade	Mother
F	1st grade	Jr. High phys. ed. teacher
G	1st grade	Mother
H	4th grade	Maternal grandfather
I	7th grade	A neighbor
J	7th grade	Mother

Each principal easily identified the grade level where they first encountered a teacher who really cared about students. Each principal easily produced the name of that teacher. While saying the name of the first caring teacher, each principal smiled in a wistful way. Remembrances of that teacher were spontaneously shared with the author. In fact, remembrances lengthened the time of each interview with the principals but the principals didn't seem to mind.

Identifying the most caring person the principal has ever known was difficult for the principals. Once the principal finally identified that person, however, a similar wistful smile appeared and remembrances were shared.

Question 5

Is there a characteristic-type pattern in the elementary principal who is responding to the negative effects of social change?

The Myers-Briggs Type Inventory, Form G, was, at the outset of the study, the primary assessment of characteristics of the ten Elementary Principals who participated in the study. Of sixteen types possible in the *MBTI,* the ten principals studied fit into eight types. From these sixteen type possibilities, four characteristic strands are formed. For example, one strand is for Introverted Perceptive Types and another strand is for Introverted Judging Types. A third strand is for Extroverted Perceptive Types and a fourth is for Extroverted Judging Types. Of the four possible strands, 50% of the Principals studied (five) fit into the Extroverted Perceptive Type. The next most common type was the Introverted Judging Type (three). One principal fit the Introverted Perceptive Type and one principal fit the Extroverted Judging Type.

A characteristic pattern could not be identified among the principals through the *Myers-Briggs* test results. An Extroverted Perceptive Type mode, however, was identified since 50% of the principals fit this type. Extroverted Perceptive Type individuals are described as active, sociable, and always seeking new experiences. They are seen as adaptable extroverts among the four major types. Of the ten principals studied, eight (80%) fit into two of the four major types: Extroverted Perceptive (five) and Introverted Judging Type (three). Introverted Judging Type individuals are described as persevering, decisive, introspective, and hard to convince.[103]

While the *Myers-Briggs* was used for identification of characteristic types, one interview question sought to identify an "academic" characteristic. The interview question asked attempted to uncover the principals' perception of themselves as academic students. These perceptions are included in Table 5 along with the *Myers-Briggs* results.

A glossary of *Myers-Briggs*-type terms is included in the Appendix.

TABLE 5

Two Principal Characteristics

Principal	Myers-Briggs Type	Principal as a student
A	ENFJ	C to A, over time
B	ISFP	C
C	ESFP	A and B
D	ENFP	B
E	ENFP	A and B
F	ISTJ	B
G	ESTP	A
H	ISFJ	B-C
I	ISTJ	F to A-B, over time
J	ENTP	A-B

The results of the *Myers-Briggs* test indicate no characteristic patterns among the ten principals in the study. Eight of ten principals, however, fit into two of four type strands. Five principals fit the Extroverted Perceptive strand and three principals fit the Introverted Judging strand.

An interview question attempted to identify a characteristic one might call "academic." The author wanted to find out how the principals perceived themselves as students. Nine of ten principals did not consider themselves "A" students.

Question 6

What is the gender, age, and experiential background of the principal who is responding to social change?

Gender

Seven principals were male; three were female. A 70% representation of males and a 30% representation of females is congruent with the gender make-up of elementary principals in the three counties studied.

For every ten elementary principals in these three counties combined, approximately seven are male and three are female.

No attempt was made to balance or to produce any proportionate representation of the two sexes. Gender, therefore, does not seem to be a factor in responsive-to-social change elementary principals.

Age

The age range of the principals studied was 36 to 58. Two principals were 40 and two were 54. Average age was 48, median age was 51. It is possible that a principal's age is a factor in responsiveness to social change since the majority of principals studied (seven) were between the ages of 47 and 58.

The majority of the principals (nine) became a principal between the ages of 30 and 37. Only one principal considered himself a "late bloomer," having decided to become a principal after more than 20 years as an elementary teacher. This principal, a male, became a principal at age 44.

Age may be a factor in a principal's responsiveness to social change as it impacts on his or her elementary school. Age as a possible factor exists because the median age of the principals studied was 51 and the median age at which they became a principal was 34. In this study, 50% of the principals were between the age of 50 and 54. In the state of Pennsylvania, only 17% of the elementary principals are between the ages of 50 and 54.[104]

Experiential Background

The principals' experiences in the field of education varied among the ten principals in the study. Variations were such that an experiential pattern did not emerge except in the expected area of the majority holding a BS in Elementary Education. The elementary principal experience ranged from three years to twenty-four years. One female principal in her twenty-second year as an elementary principal just finished her first year in a brand new school within the same district. She found the experience renewing and exciting, even though she saw an increase in social issues negatively impacting on her new school.

The most recent data on educational leaders in Pennsylvania revealed the following: 22% of the Elementary Principals have been principals 16-20 years; 25% have been principals 21-25 years; 22% have been principals for 26-30 years. Pennsylvania data and the researcher's data differ considerably in one area. In the author's study, 40% of the principals had less than 10 years of experience as an elementary principal while in Pennsylvania, only 8% had less than 10 years of experience. Also, within the entire state of Pennsylvania, only 10 principals had less than five years of experience; three of those principals participated in the researcher's three-county study.[105]

Five of the ten principals have had all their experiences as a principal in the same school. All principals who participated in the study were certified by Pennsylvania's Department of Education. Since principal certification was a criterion for participation in the study, the author could not consider this pattern a finding. As would be expected, eight principals hold undergraduate and graduate degrees in elementary education. Two of the three urban principals were graduated from college with a BS in Health and Physical Education and were physical education teachers before becoming principals. One principal was certified in multiple disciplines, namely, English, science, and guidance. None of the principals had a doctorate although three were presently enrolled in a doctoral program.

Table 6 describes the gender and age of each principal as well as years of experience as a principal.

TABLE 6

Principal's Gender, Age, and Experience

Principal	Gender	Age	Years of Experience as Principal
A	M	51	17
B	M	53	15
C	F	54	22
D	M	47	3
E	M	50	20
F	F	58	24
G	F	40	3
H	M	54	23
I	M	40	9
J	M	36	4

Gender was not a factor in this study. Age and experience, however, appear to be factors in principals who participated in this study.

While the author understands the term change agent was first defined by Grossman and applied to males in the corporate world, she also was interested in the principal as change agent. Grossman's change agent criteria of the 1970's were: young, inexperienced, and male. The principal in the study fit just one of the three change-agent criteria: male. Median age of the principals in the study was 51; average age was 48. Median for years of experience as a principal was 15 years; average years of experience was 14. The principals in the study did not meet the original change agent criteria of inexperience and youth.

Question 7

What is the basis for the principal's response to social change as it impacts on the school?

Each principal seemed able to identify with today's students who are struggling with the negative effects of social change. Even though none of the principals grew up in a single parent home nor a home where parents had remarried or lived with another adult outside of marriage, each principal seemed able to identify with the childhood struggles their students were experiencing. All principals believed they were accepting of change, even when they didn't like it. A majority reported knowing principals who were resistant to change and unproductive as a result. Nine of the principals expressed, in both verbal and nonverbal ways, that they were energetically thriving amidst social change and seized every opportunity to make a positive difference for children, teachers and families. Only one principal questioned his/her ability to continue addressing, with energy, the complexities social change was bringing his/her school.

The principals studied appear to be responding to students caught in the middle of social change because they care and are needed by their students. The principals were particularly concerned about students who were living in or near poverty conditions. Poverty or near-poverty was seen by the principals as the root of most other social problems.

The principals reported between 8% and 95% of their students received free or reduced-priced lunch. As would be expected, the principals in the urban schools reported the highest percentage of students receiving free or reduced price lunch.

The student population for which the principals were responsible ranged from 424 to 720. Four of the principals had responsibilities in more than one school. The principals studied were responsible for an average of 572 students. Table 7 indicates how many students are receiving free or reduced price lunch and in which type of school.

TABLE 7

Principal's Present School Type and Student Population

Principal School	Type of Lunch	#Students	% Free/Reduced-Price
A	Rural*	710	15%
B	Suburban	650	8%
C	Suburban	424	19%
D	Rural	476	15%
E	Suburban	460	25%
F	Urban	651	95%
G	Rural*	536	14%
H	Rural**	519	25%
I	Urban	720	85%
J	Urban*	570	40%

* responsible for 2 schools
** responsible for 3 schools

All ten principals expressed a commitment to make a positive difference for students caught in the middle of multiple social change issues. Seven of the ten principals studied cited their own negative elementary school experiences as the main reason they want to respond positively to social change as it impacts on *their* elementary school. Six of the ten principals made numerous references to their own childhood struggles with poverty or near-poverty.

The verbal responses to the author's closure question, "Why do you think you are responding to social change as it impacts on the elementary school?," are quoted below. Each principal is identified by letter name only.

Principal A: "My background influenced me. I lived in a family that really struggled during World War II with seven kids. I can identify with those who have problems. I also credit my religious faith, for the greatest teacher of all is Christ."

Principal B: "Because I care about kids I want to see them succeed. When you feel that way you need to deal with the factors that are hindering their success. You try to help them overcome."

Principal C: "I suppose because I love the kids and there is a need there. I just do what has to be done."

Principal D: "I think it is part of my nature. I respond to things like that. I think I'm bendable. I go with the flow."

Principal E: "I've always been a champion of the underdog. My family always struggled to make ends meet and I want to help my kids at school who are also struggling."

Principal F: "I think because of my own personal experiences, seeing how some educators don't respond and what happens to kids because no one did respond. I don't want to do that to kids."

Principal G: "I don't think principals have any choice. If you understand the system, you understand if you don't do it, nobody else will. Your effort has to be worthwhile. It shows when a principal isn't involved."

Principal H: "Because our society is changing. Schools reflect or mirror society as best they can in order to help the youngster. The kids are victims of their own environment. As adults, we create that environment so it's up to us to make things as positive for kids as possible."

Principal I: "I don't think we run the education system very well. I see a lot of things in this school I would still like to see changed. We are not meeting the needs of kids coming to school. They're not learning. People are resistant to change. They want to piss and moan but still do the same old thing that still doesn't work. If something's not working, you fix it and you do it within the structure."

Principal J: "Part of it has to do with the way I grew up, the way I felt about the public schools as seeing me as a nothing, a non-entity. The other people with the clout and the money in the community were responded to. They had the importance. I can't even live in the place I left. Here I think I can change some of that for kids."

Once all research questions were answered, the author sought a logical way to display her general findings. She constructed Tables 8 and 9 in order to display these findings.

Analysis of all data gathered were classified as findings either common to all principals or to the majority of principals. Table 8 describes 29 findings common to all principals who participated in the study. These findings do not fall neatly into the seven social issues identified by the author. Each of the seven social issues, however, is represented at least once in Table 8. Also represented in Table 8 are principal characteristics and activities, including experiences and self-reporting.

TABLE 8

Findings Common to All Ten Principals

Finding No.	Principal Activities and Characteristics

1. expressed concern for increase in poverty among their students
2. identified school nurse as the key person addressing poverty
3. stated needs of parents must be addressed along with their children's needs
4. spoke of dignity, anonymity and discretion when addressing children and parents living in poverty or near poverty
5. described projects on behalf of needy students
6. expressed growing concern for the youngest children, preschool to 2nd grade
7. described kindergarten screening that relates to children's educational plan
8. reported single-parent families are addressed in the curriculum
9. described flexible parent conferences, including evening conferences for parents who work daytime hours
10. saw child care as biggest problem for mothers in workforce and supported the establishment of child care programs within their school or community.
11. provided school bus transportation to a sitter's house or a day care center
12. concerned about increase in child abuse among students

TABLE 8 (continued)

Findings Common to All Ten Principals

Finding No.	Principal Activities and Characteristics

13. believed neglect is a form of child abuse and should be addressed as such byChildren and Youth Services (CYS)
14. satisfied with the way their school is handling suspected child abuse cases
15. criticized the lack of responsiveness and effectiveness of CYS
16. stated cultural diversity is a social issue that should be addressed more consciously in their schools
17. stated consequences of drug/alcohol abuse are impacting on schools
18. reported drug/alcohol prevention programs are begun by 2nd grade
19. grew up in either lower or middle class families (no upper class)
20. grew up at home with biological mother and father; experienced no divorces among their parents
21. were not second born nor classic middle of three ordinal positions
22. were married to their original spouse
23. all males had children; all females had no children
24. quickly identified their first caring teacher; immediately knew name
25. struggled to identify the most caring person they ever knew; then, did not name their first caring teacher
26. certified in Pennsylvania as elementary principals
27. had at least 3 years experience as elementary principal
28. said they can identify with today's student who is struggling with social problems
29. expressed a zeal and commitment to making a positive difference for students caught in the middle of social change

While the researcher identified 29 findings common to all principals in the study she also identified 28 findings common to the majority of principals. Six of the seven social issues identified by the researcher are represented in Table 9. The social issue of Mothers in the Workforce is the only social issue not represented.

TABLE 9

Findings Common to the Majority of Principals

Frequency	Principal Activities and Characteristics
9	revealed their school's child care plans for the future
9	were actively involved in several programs/projects aimed at drug and alcohol prevention
9	considered themselves other than "A" students
9	became a principal between the age of 30 and 37
9	expressed they were thriving amidst social change and were functioning at a high level in order to make a positive difference
8	followed different procedures when dealing with suspected physical abuse and suspected neglect cases
8	called Children and Youth Services immediately for any type of suspected child abuse
8	described in detail serious cases of child abuse this school year
8	described pre-kindergartners through second graders with fetal alcohol syndrome and fetal cocaine damage
8	fit into two of the four major type strands of the *Myers-Briggs Type Inventory, Form G*
8	held undergraduate degrees in elementary education
7	were actively involved soliciting clothing, food, and funds for school supplies, field trips and extra-curricular activities for children in need
7	demonstrated a working knowledge of the ways the single parent family and non-traditional families have become part of the elementary curriculum
7	incorporated into the curriculum the drug and alcohol program developed by the Chemical Health Education Foundation called, "Here's Looking at you, 2000"
7	did not attend the same type of elementary school their present students are attending

TABLE 9 (continued)

Findings Common to the Majority of Principals

Frequency	Principal Activities and Characteristics
7	perceived the socio-economic status of their childhood classmates as similar or very similar to the socio-economic status of their present elementary students
7	identified their own first caring teacher as being encountered in the fourth through the seventh grade
7	were between the ages of 47 and 58
7	were male
7	cited their own negative childhood experiences in elementary school as the main reason they were responding to social change as it impacts on students in their present school
6	supported with written requests (memos to staff and superiors) an aggressive seeking of funds, supplies and other assistance to children in need
6	described in detail the ways their school is addressing cultural diversity
6	began drug and alcohol prevention programs in kindergarten
6	offered special seminars for parents on drug and alcohol prevention
6	were least responsive to the social issue of cultural diversity
6	expressed difficulty in deciding to which social issue they were most responsive
6	grew up in a family they identified as having lower class socio-economic status
6	made more than one reference to their own childhood struggle with poverty or near-poverty

Data in Tables 8 and 9 can be combined for a total of 57 principal findings. While other principal activities and characteristics were found among four and five principals, the researcher limited her findings to those discovered in six or more principals.

The classification of principal activities and principal characteristics emerged from the data during the analysis phase of the study. Principal activities included the ways the principal was addressing social change issues. Principal characteristics were derived from the principal's experiences, self-reporting, demographic-type data and the *Myers-Briggs Type Indicator, Form G*. Being able to classify principal activities and characteristics assisted the researcher in creating Tables 8 and 9 for enhancement of the text. The researcher quadrupled her checking of data recording and data analysis in order to prevent researcher bias or error.

VI

What Does It All Mean?

The study examined ten elementary principals recognized as leaders responding in positive ways to the negative effects of social change as they impacted on the elementary school. The study took place in three counties in south-eastern Pennsylvania. The elementary principals in the study were identified by a panel of educational leaders in the three counties in which the study took place. Twelve elementary principals were identified by the panel as principals who were responding to social change as it impacted on their schools. Eight males and four females were identified by the panel from a potential population of sixty-eight males and twenty-eight females.

SUMMARY

The author invited all twelve identified elementary principals to participate in the study. One male principal declined because he was in the midst of closing three elementary buildings and opening a brand new school. One female principal would have accepted but the researcher had to reject her participation because she was not certified as an elementary principal in Pennsylvania. In fact, she did not hold a principal's certificate, but functioned as a principal through a supervisory certificate. In order to participate in the study, principals had to be Pennsylvania certified elementary principals and presently working as elementary principals in the public schools.

The population of the study was ten. With a population of ten, the author does not attempt to generalize her findings to the population of elementary principals in Pennsylvania. All findings, therefore, have been confined to ten principals working in three counties in south-eastern Pennsylvania.

Seven social issues were investigated with the principals who participated in the study as well as some of the principals' professional and personal experiences, including childhood experiences. The author identified the following social issues: poverty, single parent families, mothers in the workforce, child care, child abuse, cultural diversity, and drug and alcohol abuse. The author wanted to discover what the principals were doing in response to social change and the reasons why they were responding. She also wanted to identify characteristics among the ten principals who participated in the study.

The author conducted a pilot study in order to test a three-part instrument as well as her data collecting method. The pilot study took place in a Pennsylvania county different from the counties in which the actual study took place. Principals who participated in the pilot study made useful evaluative comments immediately following the interview component of the study. As a result of the evaluative comments of participants in the pilot study, the author eliminated several questions from her interview survey, decided not to use a tape recorder, maintained the Myers-Briggs Type Inventory, Form G as part of the instrument, and continued the practice of sending the *Myers-Briggs* to the principals one week in advance of the interview. As a result of the pilot study, the author made effective refinements to the instrument and improved her data collecting method.

The actual study began two weeks after the pilot study. The author conducted an in-person interview with each principal. The interview was structured to be completed in one to one-and-a half hours, although all principals continued to talk about their work after the formal interview had ended. In addition, the Myers-Briggs *Type Inventory, Form G*, was completed by each principal in advance of the interview. In all instances, the elementary principal handed the completed *Myers-Briggs* test to the author during introductory handshaking and amenities prior to the interview. The version of the Mye*rs-Briggs* test used was self-scoring; therefore, the principals knew their characteristic type score in advance of the interview. Nine principals said their score was an accurate assessment. Nine reported they enjoyed completing the test and found it non-threatening and relatively easy to complete. One principal said she found some of the questions difficult because she wanted to answer them as both a principal and a woman.

Of the ten principals participating in the study, four were principals of rural schools, three were principals of suburban schools and three were principals of urban schools. Years of experience as a principal ranged from three to twenty-four years. Median age of the principals was 51. Average number of students for whom the principal was responsible was 572. The percent of students living in or near poverty ranged from 8% to 95%.

While the author sought to identify what the principals and their schools were doing in response to social change, the heart of her study was to identify characteristics of principals who were responding. Once the author analyzed what principals were doing to respond to social change as it impacted on their schools, as well as self-reporting and demographic data, she was able to identify characteristics.

A total of 585 miles was traveled by the author in order to conduct the interviews. The longest amount of time spent talking with a principal was two-and-a-half hours. The shortest amount of time was one hour and thirty-five minutes. All interviews were conducted within a one-month time period.

DISCUSSION

The author's data revealed 29 findings common to all ten principals and 28 findings common to the majority of principals. An analysis of those combined 57 common findings revealed the social issues appearing most often were poverty, child abuse, and drug and alcohol abuse. Each of these social issues appeared seven times among common findings. Clearly, the principals found child abuse the most disturbing social issue to discuss with the author. While all ten principals claimed they were satisfied with the way their schools addressed child abuse, all ten principals also stated they were dissatisfied with the follow-through of Children and Youth Services personnel.

There was no single social issue to which the majority of principals claimed they responded most, in either frequency or intensity. When asked to select just one from the seven social change issues identified, the majority of the principals expressed an inability to do so. The principals required an inordinate amount of time to respond to the author's question and then, in four instances, selected two social issues to which they responded most instead of the requested one. The social issue to which the principals responded least was cultural diversity. The principals were quickly able to identify cultural diversity as the one social issue to which they responded least. As would be expected, the urban principals were more responsive to cultural diversity than were the rural principals.

Clearly, the principals who participated in the study were committed to making a difference for students caught in the middle of social change, both in and out of school. The author discovered all principals actively cared about their students beyond the schoolhouse door. They knew of their students' families and the socio-economic factors impacting on family life. Personal information about students, siblings, parents, grandparents and pets was information that was important to the principal. That information was used by the principal to assist, in discreet ways, the entire family.

The principals knew where students' parents worked or used to work. They knew when their students were in need of clothes, food, money, or medical care. The principals led projects aimed at helping their most needy students, those from poverty situations and non-traditional families. During the interview, the principals gave numerous examples of the practice that no child in their schools ever went "without" food or clothing or school supplies and participation in extra-curricular activities. Every principal made certain bus transportation was provided from school to the baby-sitter or child care center. Even when the school district did not necessarily approve bus transportation for meeting child care needs after school, the principal found ways to get around non-approval. Clearly, all principals who participated in the study solicited help for their students in aggressive ways. The majority of the principals felt no compunction about bending the rules or pursuing atypical or unusual means in order to provide what their students needed.

The principals who participated in the study provided flexibility with parent-teacher conferences, and made sure the needs of single parents, non-custodial parents and mothers in the workforce were met. All principals provided for evening parent conferences as well as early morning, lunchtime and late afternoon conferences. Each principal described, in detail, the kinds of flexibility provided parents who were themselves caught in the middle of social change. All principals believed parents must be made to feel welcome in school, no matter how negatively affected by social change parents themselves may be.

The principals described the many discreet or anonymous ways they gained funds, food, clothing and school supplies. Most principals' descriptions of methods employed to gain help for their students were highly creative. Their pursuits on behalf of students and families in need were unstoppable. The principals actively sought help from local businesses, churches, agencies, teachers, parents, friends, grandparents, and well-to-do citizens. One principal expressed more graphically what all principals expressed less graphically. He said, "I have one job, to educate the kids, no matter what. I'm seen as somebody who can make things happen. I go after everything I can get for the kids. Some people see me as a pain in the ass but that's OK. I want to make a difference. I believe every principal has it in him or her to make the difference."

Each principal discussed, without specifically being asked, personal projects along with children whose special needs were being addressed. The author will not mention all the children nor projects discussed by the principals, rather one or two, in order to support the study's findings through concrete examples.

Principal A made sure a fourth grade student whose family was experiencing hard times, could learn to play a musical instrument. An instrument was purchased for the child and the lessons were paid for through the efforts of the principal.

Principal B saw mental giftedness in a second grader whose eye-hand coordination was a serious problem. The principal believed a lap computer would help this child demonstrate his giftedness to others. Since the child lives in a single parent home where money is a problem, a lap computer was to be purchased for the child through the efforts of the principal. The principal said he will make sure the lap computer accompanies the child throughout his school career.

Principal C solicited funds from several unlikely sources and just purchased 39 pairs of shoes for needy students. She also asked a friend's Sunday School class to buy six food baskets for some of her students. Once this principal herself chased a habitually truant student several blocks until she caught him and returned him to school. She now allows the chasing to be done by a willing custodian.

Principal D made sure a fifth grader whose house had no heat or hot water could take showers at school. The only people aware of this practice were the principal, the school nurse and the student.

Principal E personally paid for field trips for a number of needy students when his district refused to assist. He also solicited funds from his golfing partners to pay for a drug and alcohol prevention seminar for the parents of his students.

Principal F restructures each class on a yearly basis, according to her perceptions of children's social and academic situations. Her perceptions are based on classroom observations made to analyze individual needs. Principal F also requires teachers to use current events, especially news of sports figures hurt by chemical abuse, to teach the dangers of drugs and alcohol.

Principal G discussed her involvement with a second grade student whose father was prostituting her in order to feed his drug habit. The principal pursued a successful reversal of this practice so that the second grader could attempt to be a child again.

Principal H sought help from local churches and civic groups when students' families needed to pay the coal bill or purchase food. His daily work is based on feeling responsible to be someone who helps children understand the life around them as well as the 3 R's.

Principal I described some of the 35 projects he directed over nine years as principal of an inner city school. He stated more than once that the needs of his students are so great, he cannot afford to let a single potential resource pass him by. His most recent joy from the Reading Incentive Program was a Go-Cart experience for 120 students, paid-in-full by a local business.

Principal J spoke of his efforts to restructure both of his urban schools. One of his restructuring efforts is to make both schools non-graded. Principal J saw countless inequities in the present structure of public schools, inequities which cause most harm to the student caught in the middle of social change.

All principals explicitly or implicitly revealed their commitment to protect students from anything that might hurt their dignity and pride. They talked of building student self-esteem, self-worth, and responsibility in spite of the negative effects of social change. The principals would not allow students to use social problems as excuses for anti-social behavior or poor academic performance. The principals' academic and behavioral standards for students negatively affected by social change were high. Numerous references to individual students and their academic achievement were made during the interview.

The interview method proved to be an effective way for the author to gain the information she sought. The heart of the study was to identify characteristics of principals who were responding to social change. In addition to the characteristic-type questions included in the instrument developed by the author, the Myers-Briggs Type Inv*entory, Form G,* was also used to determine whether or not a characteristic pattern existed among the principals who participated in the study.

The *Myers-Briggs Type Inventory, Form G*, was selected because it appeared relevant to the purpose of the study. It also offered extensive reliability and validity data. A 309-page manual written exclusively for researchers as a guide to the *Myers-Briggs* contains numerous studies somewhat related to the researcher's study; however, the author determined only one study could be used for comparative purposes. That study was conducted with 1,024 elementary and secondary principals. The author compared her findings with the findings of the study cited in the Myers-Bri*ggs* manual and discovered the ten principals in her study agreed with the more extensive Myers-Briggs study in two of four type strands. The author found no agreement in the remaining two type-strands. A chart that compared the researcher's findings with the larger study cited in the Myer*s-Briggs* manual is included in the Appendix. The author suggests the readers of the chart keep two variables in mind: [1] The author's study population of 10 cannot be statistically compared with the other study's population of 1,024. [2] The other study combined data collected from both elementary and secondary principals whereas the author's study was based exclusively on data collected from elementary principals. Nevertheless, the author considered the findings interesting enough to include in the Appendix.

The combination approach of the two-part interview and the use of the Myers-Briggs Type Inventory, *Form G* resulted in numerous findings. Of the 57 findings common to the principals, 32 were classified as principal activities and 25 were classified as principal characteristics. More principal characteristics were revealed through the author's demographic-type questions during the interview than through the MBTI scores. The data collected through the *MBTI* were, nevertheless, intriguing for the author to analyze and of great personal interest to each principal.

The author acknowledges she is unable to generalize her findings beyond the population of her study. Through an analysis of data gathered, however, the author was able to establish a profile of the elementary principal who is responding to social change as it impacts on his or her school. Since seven of the ten social-responsive principals in the study were male, gender references in the profile will be "he." Below is the profile.

A PROFILE OF THE ELEMENTARY PRINCIPAL WHO IS RESPONDING TO SOCIAL CHANGE

The elementary principal is married to his original spouse, and the parent of at least one child. The average age of the principal is 48 and his median age is 51. He has at least three years of experience as an elementary principal and as many as twenty-four. He holds an undergraduate degree in elementary education as well as a Pennsylvania certificate as an elementary principal. He became a principal at age 34.

The principal can identify with today's student struggling with the negative effects of social change both in and out of school. One reason for this ability to identify with students who are struggling might be the principal's own childhood experiences with poverty or near-poverty. The elementary principal who is responding to social change as it impacts on his students did not grow up in an upper-class or wealthy family. In fact, he considers himself as having grown up in a lower class socio-economic family.

Unlike the majority or growing majority of his elementary students, however, the elementary principal grew up at home with his biological mother and father, who remain or remained married to one another throughout their lifetime. The birth order position of the elementary principal was first-born, middle of a large family or youngest; he was rarely an only child. Even though the type of elementary school where he is principal is different or very different from his childhood elementary school, he, nevertheless, finds the socio-economic make-up of his elementary students similar or very similar to his childhood classmates. He knows what it is like for a child to struggle to overcome adversity, no matter what type of school a child attends.

Sometimes, the principal is responsible for students in two or three schools. The average number of students for whom he is responsible is 572. Among those students, an average of 34% are receiving free or reduced-price lunch. The percent of students living in poverty ranges from 8% to 95%.

Today, the responsive-to-social change elementary principal recalls his own elementary school experiences as rather negative. Occasionally, he expresses anger with his childhood elementary teachers. He seldom came upon his first caring teacher in the primary grades. Only rarely, did he come upon his first caring teacher before fifth grade. He cites his own negative experiences in elementary school as a clue to his determination to make elementary school experiences for all his students positive.

The elementary principal truly believes he can make a positive difference for elementary students presently struggling with the negative effects of social change, no matter how negative those effects may be. He is so determined, he will sometimes anger teachers, bend school rules and twist community arms in order to get whatever students need for physical, psychological, and academic survival. Whenever he can help the families of his students with monetary and material needs, he will.

The elementary principal does not fit neatly into one of sixteen characteristic-types on the *Myers-Briggs Type Inventory, Form G,* but rather in one of eight characteristic-types. He does appear to fit the *Myers-Briggs* Extroverted-Perceptive Type more frequently than the Introverted-Thinking Type. When asked whether he sees himself as an "A" student, he does not hesitate to reveal he struggled for grades yet still was not an "A" student. He states he is usually a "B" or "C" student which may indicate why, on the *Myers-Briggs*, he is more a Feeling Type than a Thinking Type. In spite of not being an "A" student, the responsive-to-social-change principal is intelligent and perceptive. He displays an abundance of physical and mental energy.

The social responsive elementary principal will rarely choose a teacher as the most caring person he ever knew but he will identify his mother more often than anyone else. The elementary principal who is responding to social change as it impacts on his school is a caring, dynamic, determined person who will make a positive difference for children in the areas of academics, self-discipline and self-esteem.

IMPLICATIONS

While the heart of the study was qualitative research, both qualitative and quantitative data were gathered and analyzed. Implications were gleaned from both kinds of data. Tables were provided to support and enhance the findings.

One of the strongest implications appeared to be the influence of childhood family and elementary school experiences on the principals participating in the study. The responsive-to-social-change elementary principal appears to have been influenced more by his or her own childhood and elementary school experiences than by gender or type of childhood elementary school attended. Clearly, no responsive-to-social-change principal in the study grew up in an affluent or near-affluent family. This finding suggests that responding to social change may be difficult for the principal who grew up in affluence or near-affluence.

None of the responsive-to-social-change principals in the study experienced the divorce of their parents. Yet even growing up within a family where parents did not divorce, the principal reported his or her childhood family struggled in one way or another. This finding suggests that principals who grew up in a family where parents never divorced are, nonetheless, able to identify with students growing up in one-parent and/or non-traditional families. This same finding applies to the principals' present family life. All ten principals are married and remain married to their original spouse. A common denominator for the principal and his or her students appears to be childhood socio-economic status, or as one principal stated, "Hard times." Perhaps hard times during childhood motivated these principals to respond to children who are also experiencing hard times.

The author gathered numerous clusters of principal remembrances and identified several themes. A central theme among the principals' remembrances was the perception of "overcoming adversity." Other perceived central themes among the principals were "never take 'no' as the final answer", and "there is no social excuse good enough for student misbehavior or poor grades." These themes imply the responsive-to-social change principal is, indeed, a strong-willed, determined person.

As in most studies, this study produced both expected and unexpected results. The following are among the more unexpected results:

- principals were intelligent, mentally alert, yet not "A" students
- divorce and non-traditional family structures were nonexistent during the principals' childhood years
- principals were all married, and to their original spouses
- female principals had no children; male principals had at least one child
- two of the three urban principals were former physical education teachers
- most male principals were angry about their own elementary school experiences, especially in the primary grades
- all female principals said their first caring teacher was a primary grade teacher
- all male principals said their first caring teacher was not a primary grade teacher
- the 7:3 male-female ratio of the study was identical to the gender ratio in the three Pennsylvania counties in which the study took place as well as the state itself
- all principals spoke knowledgeably about the curriculum, student performance and parent-teacher conferences
- only 12 % of the elementary principals in three Pennsylvania counties were recognized by an educational panel as being responsive to social change

The unexpected results of research studies tend to produce the most interesting and intriguing implications. This study is no exception, although discovering the expected was also intruiging and interesting, at least to the person conducting the research. With a population of ten, however, the author does not want to generalize beyond the boundaries of her study.

Common threads of personality, perception and performance appeared to weave through and connect all principals studied. The principals in the study exhibited what the researcher saw as the dynamic human qualities of assertiveness, dominance, and determination. Principal gender appeared to have no influence on those dynamic human qualities. The author perceived the female principals to be equal to male principals in dynamic human qualities. There were no proverbial shrinking violets among the ten principals studied, be they male or female. The author found herself awed by the dynamic qualities seen and felt in the principals during the in-person interview.

As is the case with most researchers, this author was disappointed that the *Myers-Briggs Type Inventory* did not produce a clear characteristic pattern among the principals studied. The second disappointment was the author's decision to conduct the study within a three-county region. In retrospect, she might have opened the study to include principals in four or five counties in Pennsylvania instead of limiting the study to three counties. By expanding geographical boundaries, the author most likely would have emerged with a larger population. Perhaps someone else will push the geographical boundaries self-imposed by the original researcher in order to uncover new knowledge of the elementary principal who is responding to social change as it impacts on his or her school. The implications of this small study appear strong enough to merit further study.

RECOMMENDATIONS

Findings that merit further study were formulated in the following questions:

[1] Would a replication of this study result in similar findings?

[2] Since the male-female ratio of the study was consistent with the male-female ratio of the population from which the sample was drawn, does this mean one sex has no "responsiveness edge" on the other sex in regard to social change in the elementary school?

[3] How are teachers, nurses, guidance counselors, and other school personnel accepting the demands of the principals who are responding to social change?

[4]   How do elementary principals who are not recognized as responding to social change compare with elementary principals who are?

[5]   What are the practices of and the relationship between school districts and Children and Youth Services in regard to child abuse?

[6]   What are principal certification programs doing to prepare the elementary principal for response to social change?

[7]   How do school districts address the concept of social change when hiring elementary principals for schools where social change has a significant negative impact on the students?

[8]   Is there a relationship between a principal's family structure and his or her response to students caught in the middle of the negative effects of social change?

[9]   Considering the inevitability of social issues impacting in negative ways on schools, what motivates an individual to want to become an elementary principal?

[10]   What is the frequency and intensity of problems within each of the social issues identified by the researcher?

The author found the above ten questions in need of answers. Most certainly, elementary school personnel will continue to address the negative effects of social change well into the 21st century. The author's belief is that the ten principals recommended for the study were correctly identified by a panel of educational leaders. While the author sensed during each principal interview that she was speaking with a caring and actively committed elementary principal, it was only during the data analysis phase that she came to realize the extent of that caring and commitment to children, especially children negatively affected by social change.

All principals who participated in the study became animated when discussing their efforts on behalf of needy students. While the principals freely and enthusiastically discussed their own efforts on behalf of students and families, the principals, nevertheless, remained modest, even unassuming, about their accomplishments. The principals gave teachers and other staff members most of the credit for their schools' efforts to address the negative effects of social change. To a person, there was a desire to let the researcher know *others* were the true force behind the principal's accomplishments. There was almost an absence of credit-seeking among the principals. Instead, there was observable pride and pleasure on the principals' faces and in their words whenever they discussed the accomplishments of their students, their students' parents, teachers, nurses and counselors. To be in the presence of such strong, dynamic, determined educational leaders who displayed an absence of large egos was quite refreshing!

The educational leader expected to deal directly with the negative effects of social change as they impact on the elementary school is the elementary principal. Elementary principals recognized for their response to social change appear to be far too few in number. Whether today's elementary principal works in a rural, suburban, or urban school, he or she is experiencing and will continue to experience the negative effects of social change as they impact on students, teachers, support staff and parents. While social change brings with it both positive and negative effects, the negative effects will continue to be of special concern and challenge to elementary principals. Elementary principals who successfully respond to the negative effects of social change will be elementary principals whose activities and characteristics resemble those described in this study.

VII

Building Blocks, Foundations and Influence

There is no way to overstate the following: the negative effect of social change is nothing new. The author's mother experienced in 1916 the social change issues her daughter would be studying in the 1990's. At age four, the author's mother was thrown abruptly into poverty and life in a single-parent family. The social issues of child care, child abuse, cultural diversity and drug and alcohol abuse followed, one-by-one, enveloping her and her siblings and trapping them in a tragic pattern. All four children in the family would have been labeled "at risk" had there been a label in 1916. Of the four children, only one would miraculously grow up mentally healthy, emotionally stable and socially responsible — the author's mother. Why? Throughout her life, the author's mother credited her elementary school teachers and principal with "saving her life."

Public school personnel can never tell for sure how much influence they have on the developing child. And so, every public school employee must move through their life's work AS IF they can, indeed, make a difference for kids, no matter how trapped they may seem to be in the web of social change issues. Public school personnel must never give up or give in!

The children of Ward and June Cleaver were never labeled "at risk" during their years as students in school. Social change issues most certainly existed but there were fewer of them, the life-span was shorter and the cumulative negative effect was minimal. While the term "at risk" emerged during the late 1960's, it was neither recognized nor accepted by most people until the late '70's and mid-'80's. Then the essay, *A Nation At Risk*, made the term "at risk" a household utterance.

The term 'at risk' was first applied to students in public schools believed to be in danger of grade retention and/or dropping out of school altogether. The term "at risk" now seems to apply to any child in danger of growing up unnurtured, underdeveloped and lacking in hope, socially-responsible values, positive attitudes and useful skills. With the expansion of the term "at risk," comes a question: Who now among this country's children is *not* "at risk"? Who among this country's children in the year 2010 will *not* be "at risk?"

Irrefutably, more and more unnurtured, underdeveloped children, lacking in hope, socially-responsible values, positive attitudes and useful skills are now students in our public schools. An even greater number is set to enter school for the first time this Fall. We met four of them earlier — remember Chad, Carrie, Marci and Felipe? In order to paint a more complete word-picture of today's children, we need to meet students ready to *leave* the elementary school to begin their secondary school experience. Meet six students who are now in their last year of public elementary school. They are 6th grade students in the school of one of the Elementary Principals who participated in the author's study. Each 6th grader exemplifies today's child growing up in a world of developmental "absences." Developmental absences are the missing character and mental and physical health building blocks *essential* to the well-being of a developing person. These essential building blocks are pretty well in place before children enter public schools as kindergartners. Their foundations are poured not by school personnel but rather by parents, relatives, guardians and other caretakers.

Before we meet those 6th graders, we need to list those six building blocks believed essential to the creation of a mentally and physically healthy person who is socially responsible as well as a positive contributor to the community and the workplace.

- emotional stability
- a sense of order to daily family life
- developmental appropriateness to daily activities
- time quantity and quality
- non-instant gratification to wants, demands and gimmes
- a sense of personal responsibility

Let's briefly examine each essential through the eyes and words of those six 6th graders.

EMOTIONAL STABILITY

Robbie

I feel restless most of the time. I need action constantly so I don't have to deal with down time. Down time would force me to think about all my problems. I'd much rather escape problems than face them. I guess I'm just like my Mom. She is always on the move, always running from something or someone. Sometimes she gets caught, mostly, she doesn't. Not getting caught has become my goal in life.

Sometimes I feel scared as hell, even though I'd never let anyone know. I have my ways of dealing with my restlessness and scarediness. I don't know what I'd do if I had to stop and face my problems. There's only one grown-up I could open up to and he's living 3,000 miles away. I'm talking about my Dad who remarried and now has a bunch of little kids with his new wife. He sends me a Christmas present every year but forgets my birthday. I'd rather he forgot me at Christmas and remembered me on my birthday. Oh well, that's life in the fast lane.

My grandfather was someone I could talk to about problems when I was a really little kid. Since he died, I mostly keep my mouth shut and my eyes wide open. I won't let problems come near me. I've got my ways.

A SENSE OF ORDER TO DAILY FAMILY LIFE

Tony

Sometimes I wake up at 7, other times 8, and still other times I sleep 'til noon. It just depends on what time I went to bed. I never go to bed the same time but I never hit the sack before midnight. The time I go to bed depends on what my mom and her boyfriend are doing. I'm not saying mom and Manny are always doing it and want me out of the way. It's just that I know when they're going to do it because they're really nice to me for about an hour before they head for the bedroom and lock the door. They give me money for a pizza and tell me I can watch an HBO movie as late as I want, even on school nights.

Last year when I was 10, my mom's boyfriend was Herbie. I liked Herbie because he used to take me along with him to bars even when mom wasn't along. He'd give me quarters for the shuffleboard and I'd have a good time by myself while he drank and laughed with the guys. Now when I see Herbie on the street he acts like he hates me. He shoves his fist near my face and says, 'You and your mom are both shit.' I'm hoping when mom and Manny break up Manny will still say hello to me. It's hard to start liking one of her boyfriends because I never know how long they'll stay together.

I'm never sure whether to make supper or if mom will be bringing home hot wings and fries. Mom gets so mad at me whenever I think she's bringing home supper but she's not. Then she screams at me for about an hour. She used to hit and kick me around when I was younger. She knows better these days. I surprised her with a return punt last year and that ended that. By the time I'm 12, she'll probably be scared even to yell at me. I hope so.

DEVELOPMENTAL APPROPRIATENESS
TO DAILY ACTIVITIES

Kendra

Yesterday my friend Keisha said my mom is like a stage mother. I didn't know what Keisha meant so I asked my teacher. My teacher's definition of a stage mother sounded exactly like my mom! Anyway, my mom wants me to be a professional dancer and a classical pianist. She also wants me to be a beautician because then I can take care of my own hair, nails and make-up when I perform on stage. And so, all my life — I'm 12 now — I've been taking tap, ballet and acrobatics. Next week I will compete at Atlantic City. Mom put me on a diet last month because she said it's better for me to be on the thin side then on the fleshy side. When my diet bombed, Mom put me on diet pills. She also told me to force vomiting right after lunch at school. She said if I don't care about the way I look in my tights, at least she will.

Competing on stage scares me to death. My Mom gives me a tranquilzer an hour before I compete and that helps a little.

You know what I wish? I wish I could live at Keisha's house where the kids do normal kid things and eat normal kid things. I'd also like to come home from school just once and not have to hurry up, change and go to one of my lessons. When I grow up, I'll never be a stage mother. That's a promise.

TIME QUANTITY AND QUALITY

T.J.

The worst thing my parents ever did was to take a course called, 'Quality Time.' At this course, the instructor told my parents it's not the amount of time they spend with their children that's important but rather the quality of time they spend. That's the dumbest thing I ever heard. How can grown-ups really believe that shit? I mean, it's impossible to have quality time if you're not around your kids long enough to get to know them. My brother and I feel like our parents are strangers. They both have their careers which are obviously more important to them than their sons.

Every Saturday from 2 to 4 p.m. we have what our parents call Quality Time. It's the only time all four of us are together at the same time. We sit around the dining room table, look at each other, try hard to begin a conversation, and drink Pepsi. Mostly, we just look at each other and drink Pepsi because there's nothing to say our parents would find interesting. For example, my brother wanted to talk about a kid who brought a knife to school but my parents said they didn't want to hear about trivial things. Instead, they wanted to know my brother's thoughts about the lowering of interest rate on CD's. My brother, who is 14 said he already bought two new CDs at the record shop for the low rate of seven bucks apiece. When my father realized my brother did not know the difference between a Certificate of Deposit and a Compact Disc, he almost had a stroke. My brother got reamed out for being stupid and for the school not teaching anything important like economics and stuff like that. By 4 pm, my brother and I were so happy when Quality Time for the week was over. Two hours of quality time each week are two hours too many. I wish my parents would just spend time with us, talking, laughing, watching TV, going to baseball games and evening school events.

But then, that would mean quantity *and* quality time and my parents can afford just two quality hours a week for us kids.

NON-INSTANT GRATIFICATION TO WANTS, DEMANDS AND GIMMES

Breann

My parents both work hard at their jobs. Whoops! I'm not supposed to call them "jobs." I'm supposed to call them "professions." Pardon me! Anyway, they're proud of whatever it is they do. I hardly ever see them except when we go to the Mall or out to eat. My sister and I know how to work things so we get extra stuff whenever we're out with our parents. We lay on the guilt thing and it works every time. It works this way. We're walking through the Mall and I see a leather coat I'd like. I ooo and ah and beg to touch the coat. Mom and Dad give in and let me touch the coat. Then I say, 'Oh, I've just got to have this. Hillary got one just like it last week in camel but I'd love this black one.' I find one in my size and put it on. Of course I look like a million bucks and say so. My Dad says that's probably what it costs. I look at the price tag and tell him, no, it's 50% off. Dad asks, 'Off what?" When he hears it's 50% off $500 he starts fuming. I start pouting, then I get a little teary. I tell him his little girl hardly ever gets to see him and surely he wants to make it up to her in some way. I let him know Hillary's Dad doesn't have nearly as good a job as he does, yet Hillary's Dad is so crazy about his daughter he bought her a coat without putting up a fight.

Anyway, I got the coat that night and my younger sister got a new Barbie and a Barbie Porche. We sang in the car all the way home. As usual, our parents rode home is pissed-off silence. My sister and I don't care. We always get what we want, when we want it. That's all that matters.

A SENSE OF PERSONAL RESPONSIBILITY

Alyssa

We're studying the 'Me Generation' in social studies class. It's kind of interesting. We're studying about how too many people in this world care only about themselves and how responsibility and concern for others seem to be missing traits. People's behavior fascinates me. For example, Jamal who sits next to me in class uses the losers of the class to do his dirty work. He doesn't care how he embarrasses and humiliates others just so long as he feels like a king. Shelli who sits in front of me is always hitting on somebody for a loan that she never pays back. She doesn't care if she hurts a friend's wallet just so her wallet's full.

I might not have any children. I'm worried about pollution and the destruction of the rainforest so I plan to work in the Everglades and also South America. I'll be pretty busy cleaning up the environment and saving the rainforest. But if I *do* have children, I will teach them to feel personal responsibility for all their actions. Their wants might be in conflict with the needs and rights of others. I will help my children see how what they want may have to be put on the back burner until the time is right. I will make sure my kids know they will have to make some sacrifices for the good of the family. I will make sure they follow rules for good behavior. I will make sure they care at least as much about others as they care about themselves. I will help them become the 'We Generation.' I will help my own children bury the 'Me Generation.' And the world will be a much better place than it is now with all these selfish, self-centered people in it.

I wish my parents belonged to the "We Generation."

While the original Ward and June Cleaver family model of the 1950's never was as ideal as nostalgia would have us believe, still, it offered children in families basic essentials often missing in today's families.

Today, Ward and June Cleaver's grandchildren are in school. Indeed, rumor has it that their first great-grandchild is ready to enter kindergarten! What kind of parents are the contemporary Cleavers? What kind of family life are they creating for their children? In family values and parenting skills, would the Cleaver anscestors earn an A on their report card?

In far too many of today's families, parents are simply not effective parents. Their parenting skills and family values are often poorly developed, even non-existent. While life is often very hard for some parents, a hard life is never a good enough excuse to neglect, ignore, violate, disregard, misuse, pamper, or throw away one's children. In fact, there is no life situation tough enough for parents to use as an excuse for bad or ineffective parenting.

Neglecting, ignoring, violating, disregarding, misusing, pampering or throwing away one's children are all forms of child abuse. Our society appears to be tolerating such abuse. Beyond the abortion issue, there is no shouting in the streets or other forms of pro-child demonstrations. It is ironic that the only pro-child demonstrations appearing throughout the country have nothing whatsoever to do with today's outside-the-womb *children*! Far too many children today are damaged for life before they reach school age. What kind of future can be expected for young children who, if they were products manufactured for profit, would be indelibly labeled, "Damaged Goods."?

Far too many people who are now already parents are sending to school children who do not feel valued, worthy of love, hopeful, responsible for their behavior, eager and able to learn and grow and make useful contributions to their world. Until this positive social change miracle occurs and spreads across the country, public education will just have to continue responding to the complex needs of children, needs formerly met by their parents and extended families. Like it or not, the building blocks essential to human growth and development — emotional stability, a sense of order to daily life, appropriateness to daily activities (including appropriate adult *expectations*), time quantity as well as quality, non-instant gratification to demands and a sense of personal responsibility for one's behavior — will continue to fill the hands, hearts and minds of public school educators. The public school educator at the head of the pack in the elementary school is the Principal. Ready or not, like it or not, the heaviest burden of all rests on the shoulders, mind and heart of the Principal.

Will the Principal be helped along the way with the strengthening of the family? Will those six essentials missing from the lives of far too many children eventually find their way home? Is it possible those missing essentials are merely AWOL and will reappear in a new form, perhaps a higher quality form? Can the public school require parenting education courses for the parents of troubled and troublesome students? Are the negative effects of social change temporary or permanent? When will the public school know exactly how far to go in addressing the negative effects of social change as they impact on students, families and teachers? Is there an imaginary social change line that the public school must never cross over?

Today's and tomorrow's elementary principal will have to address these questions. There is no escape for the leader of the elementary school in addressing and responding to the social issues that combined and compounded to create this almost incomprehensible behemoth called "social change."

For the elementary principal who cares enough about other people's kids in order to build bridges, climb mountains, swim murky oceans and jump hurdles, the title, Elementary Principal, will fit perfectly.

Notes

[1]Children's Defense Fund, The State of America's Children (Washington, DC, 1995), 120.

[2]Children's Defense Fund, 101.

[3]Children's Defense Fund, 38.

[4]*Webster's New World Dictionary* (NY: Prentice Hall, 1991), 1075.

[5]*Webster's*, 1072.

[6]Thomas J. Sergiovanni and Robert J. Starratt, *Supervision: Human Perspectives* (NY: McGraw-Hill Book Co., 1988), 386.

[7]*Phi Delta Kappan*, April 1995, cover.

[8]Center on National Education Policy, *Do We Still Need Public Schools?* (Washington, DC, 1996), 7.

[9]Nel Noddings, *Caring* (Berkeley: Univ. of Calif. Press, 1984), 181.

[10]Noddings, 172.

[11]Noddings, 173.

[12]Albert Shanker, "The End of the Traditional Model of Schooling — and a Proposal for Using Incentives to Restructuring Our Public Schools," *Phi Delta Kappan*, January 1991, 345.

[13]Center on National Education Policy, 8.

[14]Children's Defense Fund, 18.

[15]Children's Defense Fund, 138.

[16]*The State of the World's Children 1995* (Oxford Univ. Press for UNICEF), 65.

[17]Children's Defense Fund, 42.

[18]Who's Minding the Children?" *Harvard Education Letter* (Nov/Dec 1988).

[19]Dianne F. Bradley, "Alcohol and Drug Education in the Elementary School," *Elementary School Guidance and Counseling*, Vol. 23, No. 2, December 1988, 99-105.

[20]National Survey on Drug Abuse, 1994

[21]National Parents' Resource Institute for Drug Education, "1994-95 Summary," 1995.

[22]Children's Defense Fund, 2.

[23]Martin Finkel, MD, "Sexual Abuse: A National Disgrace," at a seminar for the Reading Hospital and Medical Center, Reading, PA, September 28, 1988.

[24]Children's Defense Fund, 72-73.

[25]Children's Defense Fund, 18.

[26]Children's Defense Fund, 109.

[27]FBI Uniform Crime Reports, Hennyepen County Attorney's Office, Justice Dept., 1995.

[28]U.S. Bureau of Census, Current Population Reports, September 1995.

[29]Achy Obejas, "Latino U.S. Is Own Melting Pot," *Reading Eagle*, April 21, 1996.

[30]*Information Legislative Services*, Vol. 34, No. 11, March 22, 1996, 16.

[31]Gladys C. Noya, et al, editors, *Shifting Histories: Transforming Education for Social Change*, Harvard Educational Review, 1995, 9.

[32]Ulric Neisser, et al, "Intelligence: Knowns and Unknowns," *American Psychologist* (Harvard Educational Review, 1995), 88.

[33]Anne C. Lewis, "Questions and Answers About School Leadership, *Phi Delta Kappan*, April 1996, 525.

[34]Kozol, Jonathan, *Amazing Grace: The Lives of Children and the Conscience of a Nation* (NY: Crown Publishers, 1995), 243.

[35]Dode Morgan-Worsham, "The Dilemma for Principals," *Achievement Testing in the Early Grades* (Washington, DC: NAEYC, 1990), 64-66.

[36]Lawrence M. DeRidder, "School Dropout Prevention Begins in the Elementary Years," *Education* (Vol. 108, No. 4, 1988), 25.

[37]DeRidder, 25.

[38]Lawrence Kohlberg, *Child Psychology and Childhood Education: A Cognitive-Developmental View* (NY and London: Longman, 1987), 370.

[39]Kohlberg, 377.

[40]Deborah M. Cohen, "Elementary Principals Issue Standards for Early Childhood Program Quality," *Education Week*, August 1990, 14.

[41]Elliot Seif, "How to Create Schools That Thrive in Chaotic Times," *Educational Leadership*, Vol. 47, No. 8, May 1990, 81.

[42]Seif, 82.

[43]Bruce Joyce, Ed., "The Principal's Role in Teacher Development," *Changing School Culture Through Staff Development* (Washington DC: Association for Supervision and Curriculum Development, 1990), 71.

[44]Noddings, 173.

[45]Alfie Kohn, "Caring Kids: The Role of the School," *Phi Delta Kappan*, March 1991, 505.

[46]Kohn, 498.

[47]Kohn, 499.

[48]Policy Center Network, *State Policy and the School Principal: A Summary of Case Studies from Seven States* (Denver, CO: 1990), 13.

[49]Jane C. Lindle, Ed., et al, "Fact or Fiction: The Principal as Instructional Leader," *Pennsylvania Educational Leadership 1990-91 Yearbook*, PASCD, 49-51.

[50]Isabel Briggs Myers and Mary H. McCaulley, *Manual: A Guide to the Development and Use of the Myers-Briggs Type Indicator* (Palo Alto, CA: Consulting Psychological Press, Inc., 1990), 227.

[51]Myers-Briggs and McCaulley, 13.

[52]Myers-Briggs and McCaulley, 139.

[53]Myers-Briggs and McCaulley, 282.

[54]Myers-Briggs and McCaulley, 280.

[55] Neil Postman and Charles Weingartner, *Teaching as a Subversive Activity* (NY: Delacorte Press, 1969), 207.

[56]Postman and Weingartner, 208.

[57]Deborah M. Cohen, "We Became the Hopes and Dreams of All," *Education Week*, 1 February 1989, 6.

[58]David Elkind, "School and Family in the Postmodern World," *Phi Delta Kappan*, September 1995, 8.

[59]Elkind, 14.

[60]Joyce, 244.

[61]Joyce, 245.

[62]Lee Grossman, *The Change Agent* (NY: American Management Assoc., 1974), 10.

[63]Grossman, 10-23.

[64]Mark E. Hanson, *Educational Administration and Organization Behavior* (Newton, MA: Allyn and Bacon, Inc., 1985), 307.

[65]Hanson, 290.

[66]Hanson, 300.

[67]Sally Reed and R. Craig Sautter, "Children of Poverty: The Status of 12 Million Young Americans," *Phi Delta Kappan*, June 1990, K7.

[68]Reed and Sautter, K8.

[69]Beverly D. Payne and David A. Payne, "The Ability of Teachers to Identify Academically At-Risk Elementary Students," *Journal of Research in Childhood Education*, Vol. 5, No. 2, Spring/Summer 1991, 119-124.

[70]Payne and Payne, 121-122.

[71]Walter R. Borg and Meredith D. Gall, *Educational Research* (NY and London: Longman, Inc., 1989), 331.

[72]Borg and Gall, 5.

[73]Paul D. Leedy, *Practical Research: Planning and Design* (NY: Macmillan Publishing Co., Inc., 1980), 126.

[74]Robert M. S. Travers, *An Introduction to Educational Research* (London: Macmillan Co., 1969), 87.

[75]Leedy, 99.

[76]Richard C. Sweetland and Daniel J. Keyser, *Tests* (Austin, TX: Pro-Ed, 1990), 199-200.

[77]Myers-Briggs and McCaulley, 11-19.

[78]Daniel Meier, "A Visit with Bruno Bettelheim," *Education Week*, 9 May 1990, 56.

[79]Borg and Gall, 397.

[80]Sharan B. Merriam, *Case Study Research in Education: A Qualitative Approach* (CA: Jossey-Bass, 1988), 86.

[81]Merriam, 78-79.

[82]Pennsylvania Department of Education, in a phone call to Division of Data Services, August 1994.

[83]Borg and Gall, 402-404.

[84]Borg and Gall, 393.

[85]Travers, 87-88.

[86]Borg and Gall, 408.

[87]Myers-Briggs and McCaulley, 163-174.

[88]Myers-Briggs and McCaulley, 162.

[89]Myers-Briggs and McCaulley, 177-206.

[90]Myers-Briggs and McCaulley, 175.

[91]Merriam, 73-76.

[92]Leedy, 99.

[93]David M. Fetterman, Ed., *Ethnography in Educational Evaluation* (CA: Sage Publications, Inc., 1984), 31.

[94]Judith Goetz and Margaret D. LeCompte, *Ethnography and Qualitative Design in Educational Research* (Academic Press, Inc.: Harcourt Brace Jovanovich, 1984), 129.

[95]Leedy, 98-99.

[96]Borg and Gall, 405-405.

[97]Merriam, 80-82.

[98]Borg and Gall, 455.

[99]Leedy, 100.

[100]Leedy, 71.

[101]Noddings, 173.

[102]Leedy, 71.

[103]Myers-Briggs and McCaulley, 32-33.

[104]Pennsylvania Department of Education, in a phone call to Division of Data Services, August 1994.

[105]Pennsylvania Department of Education, in a phone call to Division of Data Services, August 1994.

Appendix A

ELEMENTARY PRINCIPALS AND SOCIAL CHANGE

PART I, PRINCIPAL PERCEPTION OF THE SCHOOL'S RESPONSE TO SOCIAL CHANGE

The researcher will say the following:

I have identified seven major social issues impacting on the elementary school: poverty, single parent families, mothers in the workforce, child care, child abuse, cultural diversity, and drug and alcohol abuse. (FOR VISUAL REFERENCE DURING THE INTER- VIEW, THE RESEARCHER WILL NOW PROVIDE PRINCIPAL WITH A GRAPHIC, LISTING THE ABOVE SOCIAL CHANGE ISSUES.)

There are no right or wrong answers to the questions I'm about to ask. Let your responses flow freely, without reservation. Do not hesitate to ask me to clarify my questions. Neither your name nor your school will be identified in my study. **You are not expected to be able to respond to all questions asked.**

Through procedures, programs and staff development, what is your school doing to respond to these issues as they impact on children, teachers, and parents?

1. Children living in or near poverty
    • health and nutrition?
    • financial assistance for field trips, school supplies, extra-curricular activities?
    • Head Start Program?
    • other preschool programs? What kind?
    • kindergarten readiness screening?
    • is entrance to kindergarten based on screening results?

2. Single parent families
   • does your curriculum provide for recognition and acceptance of the non-traditional family? How?
   •child care?
   • flexible parent conferences for parents who work during daytime hours?
   • Sitter service so parent can attend school functions?
3. Mothers in the workforce
   • child care?
   • flexible parent conferences?
   • sitter service during parent conferences and other functions?
4. 'Child Care
   • does your school operate a child care program? If not, why not? If "yes," describe your child care program
   • how are requests for transporting children to and/or from a sitter's house handled?
5. Child abuse
   • how is suspected physical child abuse handled? (includes sexual abuse)
   • are you satisfied with the results of the way your school handles suspected child abuse? Why?
   • is the child abuse of neglect handled differently from physical abuse? How?
6. Cultural diversity
   • how is your curriculum reflecting cultural diversity?
   • how does your staff demonstrate acceptance of cultural differences among students and their families?
7. Drug and alcohol abuse
   • is an effort being made to educate the family about drugs and alcohol? How?
   • how are students being educated about drugs and alcohol?
   • in which grade does drug and alcohol prevention education begin?
   • in which grade does drug and alcohol intervention begin?

PART II, THE PRINCIPAL: PERSONAL, PROFESSIONAL AND DEMOGRAPHIC TYPE DATA

A. If you had to select the social issue to which you, as a Principal, are **most** responsive, would you choose: poverty, single parent families, mothers in the workforce, child care, child abuse, cultural diversity or drug and alcohol abuse?

B. If you had to select the social issue to which you, as a Principal, are **least** responsive, would you choose: poverty, single parent families, mothers in the workforce, child care, child abuse, cultural diversity or drug and alcohol abuse?

C. In what grade did you first come upon the teacher who really cared about students?

D. Who is the most caring person you ever knew?

E. Sex: _____ male _____ female

F. Age: ____

G. Experience as elementary principal: ____ yrs.

H. Experience in this elementary school: ____ yrs.

I. School is primarily: ____Urban ____ Suburban ____ Rural

J. Number of students _____

K. Number (or percent) on free or reduced lunch _____

L. When you attended elementary school, was your school
____Urban ____Suburban ____Rural

M. How would you compare the socio-economic status of your childhood school classmates with that of your present school's students? very similar, similar, different, very different

N. How would you describe the socio-economic status of the family in which you grew up? (middle class, upper class, lower class)

O. Describe the family structure in which you grew up by naming each family member from oldest to youngest. (parents and siblings only, unless grandparent or other adult family member raised the children)
Oldest _____

_____

_____

Youngest _____

P. Would you describe yourself as an *A student,* a *B student* or something other than *A* or *B*?

Q. What education certificates do you hold?

R. Do you have children? (If no, ask, "Are you married?") (If yes,
     ask, Describe their family structure by naming family members
     from oldest to youngest") Note: "family members" as explained in
     Question O:
     Oldest   _____

                               _____
                               _____
     Youngest   _____
S. Why do you think you are responding to social change as it impacts
     on the elementary school?

CLOSURE QUESTION
     • Is there anything else you'd like to tell me about yourself or your
       work that would help me with my study?

PART III, MYERS-BRIGGS TYPE INVENTORY, FORM G

     The principal will be asked to complete this 94 item assessment in
advance of the interview. The researcher will collect the completed
MBTI at the time of the interview. A self-scoring version of the *MBTI*
will be used. Should principals have questions about their scores, the
researcher will assist in clarifying those scores.

Post Interview Telephone Call
     Within one week after the interview, the researcher will communi-
cate with the principal. Communication will be either by telephone or
by U.S. mail.
     In the following sequential order, the researcher will:
           1. Thank the Principal for participating in the study.
           2. Ask the Principal if he or she would like to add, delete,
clarify or modify anything stated during the interview.
           3. If necessary, ask the Principal to clarify information
gathered during the interview.
           4. Remind the Principal that confidentiality/anonymity reigns
           5. Remind the Principal that a copy of the study will be
provided, at the Principal's request.
     RESEARCHER'S NOTES:

Appendix B

Intermediate Unit Map

(Please see Pp. 114-115)

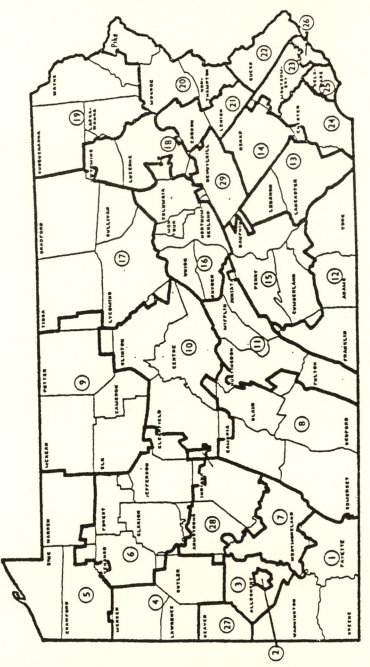

INTERMEDIATE UNITS

Commonwealth of Pennsylvania

1. Intermediate Unit 1
2. Pittsburgh-Mount Oliver
3. Allegheny
4. Midwestern
5. Northwest Tri-County
6. Clarion Manor

8. Appalachia
9. Seneca Highlands
10. Central
11. Tuscarora
12. Lincoln
13. Lancaster-Lebanon

15. Capital Area
16. Central Susquehanna
17. Blast
18. Luzerne
19. Northeastern Educational
20. Colonial Northampton

22. Bucks County
23. Montgomery County
24. Chester County
25. Deleware County
26. Philadelphia
27. Beaver Valley

Appendix C

Myers-Briggs Data Bank Sample/Comparison

Myers-Briggs Types: Principals

	ISTJ	ISFJ	INFJ	INTJ	Strand Total
data bank	12.50%	7.42%	3.91%	5.27%	29.10%
this study	20.00%	10.00%	0.00%	0.00%	30.00%
	ISTP	**ISFP**	**INFP**	**INTP**	
data bank	1.46%	2.64%	5.37%	2.54%	12.01%
this study	0.00%	10.00%	0.00%	0.00%	10.00%
	ESTP	**ESFP**	**ENFP**	**ENTP**	
data bank	2.44%	2.73%	9.28%	3.71%	18.16%
this study	10.00%	10.00%	20.00%	10.00%	50.00%
	ESTJ	**ESFJ**	**ENFJ**	**ENTJ**	
data bank	13.18%	10.55%	8.40%	8.59%	40.72%
this study	0.00%	0.00%	10.00%	0.00%	10.00%

NOTE: data bank percentages represent 1,024 elementary and secondary principals whose MBTI scores are now part of the MBTI
computer bank. MBTI has more than 250,000 scores in its data
bank.

Bibliography

Borg, Walter R. and Merideth D. Gall. *Educational Research.* New York and London: Longman, Inc., 1989.

Bradley, Dianne F. "Alcohol and Drug Education in the Elementary School." *Elementary School Guidance and Counseling*, Vol. 23, No. 2.

Center on National Education Policy. *Do We Still Need Public Schools?* Washington, D.C.: 1996.

Children's Defense Fund. *The State of America's Children.* Washington, D.C.: National Association for the Education of Young Children, 1995.

Cohen, Deborah L. Elementary Principals Issue Standards for Early Childhood Program Quality." *Education Week*, 1 Aug. 1990.

DeRidder, Laurence M. "School Dropout Prevention Begins in the Elementary Years." *Education*, vol. 108, no. 4 (Summer 1988).

Elkind, David. "School and Family in the Postmodern World." *Phi Delta Kappan*, September 1995.

Fetterman, David M., Ed. *Ethnography in Educational Evaluation.* CA: Sage Publications, Inc., 1984.

Finkel, Martin, MD. "Sexual Abuse: A National Disgrace." Seminar for the Reading Hospital and Medical Center. Reading, PA: 28 Sept. 1988.

Goetz, Judith P. and Margaret D. LeCompte. *Ethnography and Qualitative Design in Educational Research.* New York: Harcourt, Brace, Jovanovich, 1984.

Grossman, Lee. *The Change Agent.* New York: American Management Assoc., 1974.

Hanson, E. Mark. *Educational Administration and Organizational Behavior.* Newton, MA: Allyn and Bacon, Inc., 1985.

Joyce, Bruce, Ed. "The Principal's Role in Teacher Development." Changing School Culture Through Staff Development.. Alexandria, VA: Association for Supervision and Curriculum Development, 1990.

Kohlberg, Lawrence M. *Child Psychology and Childhood Education: A Cognitive-Developmental View.* NY and London: Longman, 1987.

Kohn, Alfie. "Caring Kids: The Role of the School." *Phi Delta Kappan,* March 1991.

Kozol, Jonathan. *Amazing Grace: The Lives of Children and the Conscience of a Nation.* NY: Crown Publishers, 1995.

Leedy, Paul D. *Practical Research: Planning and Design.* NY: Macmillan Publishing Co., Inc., 1980.

Lewis, Anne C. Questions and Answers About School Leadership. *Phi Delta Kappan,* April 1996.

Lindle, Jane C., Ed., Rachael Heath, et al. "Fact or Fiction: The Principal as Instructional Leader." *Pennsylvania Educational Leadership*, 1990-91 Yearbook.

Merriam, Sharan B. *Case Study Research in Education: A Qualitative Approach.* CA: Jossey-Bass, 1988.

Meier, Daniel. "A Visit With Bruno Bettelheim." *Education Week,* 9 May 1990.

Morgan-Worsham, Dode. "The Delimma for Principals." *Achievement Testing in the Early Grades.* Washington, DC, NAEYC, 1990.

Myers, Isabel Briggs and Mary H. McCaulley. *Manual: A Guide to the Development and Use of the Myers-Briggs Type Indicator.* CA: Consulting Psychologists Press, Inc., 1990.

National Parents' Resource Institute for Drug Education. *1994-95 Summary,* 1995.

Neisser, Ulric, et al. "Intelligence: Knowns and Unknowns." *American Psychologist,* Harvard Educational Review, 1995.

Noddings, Nel. *Caring.* Berkeley, CA: University of California Press, 1984.

Noya, Gladys C., et al. *Shifting Histories: Transforming Education for Social Change.* Harvard Educational Review, 1995.

Obejas, Achy. "Latino U.S. Is Own Melting Pot." *Reading Eagle,* April 21, 1996.

Payne, Beverly D. and David A. Payne. "The Ability of Teachers to Identify Academically At-Risk Elementary Students." *Journal of Research in Childhood Education,* Vol. 5, No. 2, 1991.

Pennsylvania Department of Education. Harrisburg, PA: Division of Data Services, Aug. 1994.

Pennsylvania School Boards Association. *Information Legislative Service,* Vol. 34, No. 11, March 22, 1996.

The Policy Center Network. "State Policy and the School Principal: A Summary of Case Studies from Seven States." Denver, CO: Education Commission of the States, Feb. 1990.

Postman, Neil and Charles Weingartner. *Teaching as a Subversive Activity.* NY: Delacorte Press, 1969.

Reed, Sally and R. Craig Sautter. "Children of Poverty." *Phi Delta Kappan,* June 1990.

Seif, Elliot. "How to Create Schools that Thrive in Chaotic Times." *Educational Leadership*, Vol. 47, No. 8, May 1990.

Sergiovanni, Thomas J. and Robert J. Starratt. *Supervision: Human Perspectives.* NY: McGraw-Hill Book Co., 1988.

Shanker, Albert. "The End of the Traditional Model of Schooling — and a Proposal for Using Incentives to Restructure Our Public Schools." *Phi Delta Kappan,* Jan. 1990.

Sweetland Richard C. and Daniel J. Keyser. *Tests.* Austin, TX: Pro-ed, 1990.

Travers, Robert M.W. *An Introduction to Educational Research.* London: MacMillan Co., 1969.

UNICEF. *The State of the World's Children 1995.* Oxford Univ. Press, 1995.

U.S. Bureau of Census. *Current Population Reports.* Washington, DC, 1995.

U.S. Bureau of Census. *National Survey on Drug Abuse.* Washington, DC, 1995.

U.S. Justice Department. *FBI Uniform Crime Reports.* Hennyepen County Attorney's Office, 1995.

Webster New World Dictionary. NY: Prentice Hall, 1991.

Index